Investing for Beginners

Start With $0, Pick Winning Growth Stocks and Do It All With Zero Hassle.

Mike Hartley

Mike Hartley

© **Copyright 2023 - All rights reserved.**

The content of this book may not be reproduced, copied, or transmitted without explicit written permission from the author(s) or publisher. Doing so would constitute a breach of copyright law and could result in serious legal repercussions for any party participating in the illicit reproduction of the material. Furthermore, due to the nature of intellectual rights, it is impossible to duplicate or replace the original work produced by the author(s) or publisher; therefore, the only way to legally gain access to this content is through direct authorization from either party.

The publisher and the author(s) of this book shall not be held accountable in any way for any damages, reparations or financial losses that may arise because of the information contained herein, either directly or indirectly. This includes any potential harm, monetary loss, or other consequences from individuals' usage of said information. It is also understood that these individuals will not be able to use this clause to evade legal responsibility for their wrongdoings related to the content provided in this book. The publisher and author(s) will thus be free from all liabilities associated with the publication and distribution of this book.

Legal Notice:

This book is subject to copyright protection and should only be used for personal use. Furthermore, it should not be shared with any other individual or persons for any purpose other than that for which it was initially intended. It is strictly prohibited to amend, reproduce, distribute, utilize, quote, or paraphrase any part of the content within this publication without prior authorization from the writer or publisher. Any violation of these regulations may result in legal action against those who have breached them.

Mike Hartley

Disclaimer Notice:

The presented work is strictly informational and should not be interpreted as an offer to buy or sell any form of security, instrument, or investment vehicle. Furthermore, the information contained herein should not be taken as a legal, tax, accounting or investment recommendation given by the author(s) or any affiliated company, employees, or paid contributors. In other words, the information is presented without considering individual preferences for specific investments in terms of risk parameters. It is general information that does not account for a person's lifestyle and financial objectives. It is important to note that no tailored advice will be provided based on the given information.

The authors and their parent company, along with all employees and paid contributors, have agreed to abstain from trading any stock or investment written about for at least two days publication of any new article, book, report, or email. This includes any equity, options, debt, or other instruments related to that security, stock, or company, except for existing orders that pre-existed the submission; all such charges will be disclosed inside the document. The author(s) may have direct or indirect positions in some of the companies mentioned because of holdings in mutual funds, exchange-traded funds, closed-end funds, or other similar vehicles. Such indirect holdings are usually not disclosed as there is no guarantee that the author(s) is aware at any given time of the individual portfolios of any of these funds. Furthermore, certain decisions by these funds, such as buying or selling stocks, could potentially impact an author's position even if it was not done directly by them.

Warning:

There is no simple, easy way to become wealthy, especially regarding investments in the financial markets. While it may be possible to make a significant return on your investment, there is also a high risk of losing a large amount of money if you do not have the proper knowledge and knowledge base. You must conduct thorough research and analysis to succeed with investments with the most significant potential for price appreciation. Investing wisely requires an extensive level of education and an understanding of how markets work for one's portfolio to yield positive returns over time. Before venturing into any investment endeavor, it is essential to consult an experienced financial advisor or professional who can advise what steps should be taken and how much capital should be invested. It is also necessary to review all relevant information about potential investments, such as the company's financial statements and prospectus, to make an informed decision regarding whether to invest. Everyone must remember that past results are not necessarily indicative of future performance, so it is wise never to invest more money than you can afford to lose.

This work is based upon a thorough analysis of SEC filings, current news events, interviews, corporate press releases, and knowledge obtained through our experience as financial traders, investors, journalists, and educators. We encourage readers to be careful when making decisions involving their finances, as they are ultimately responsible for the outcomes of their choices. To ensure they have thoroughly informed themselves before making any investment decisions, we strongly advise readers to take the time to research each subject in more detail by seeking out additional sources such as third-party analysts or other reading materials on the web. Furthermore, we recommend conducting a comprehensive review of all available data to ensure each conclusion is well-rounded and sound by exploring multiple aspects of an issue or topic. Ultimately, we believe that a person's financial future will benefit from making prudent and informed decisions based on knowledge gathered from various sources.

The author(s) and any parent companies may be affiliated with certain investments offered. If any of these affiliate offers are made, it will be clearly stated, however, that such affiliation exists. It is worth noting that we do not, and would never, affiliate ourselves with companies that do not meet our high standards and ideals; we would not promote anything that we wouldn't consider ourselves, and in that vein, we aim to keep any affiliations with companies that we believe to be of considerable value to our readers, subscribers, and fans. We value your time and education and try our utmost only to offer the highest quality support.

All trademarks, whether registered or pending, are the property of their respective owners.

Foreword to the Series

Investing is a necessary and invaluable life skill that many people don't even realize they need. It allows you to create financial stability, accomplish your most ambitious goals, and secure your future. Whether it be providing for loved ones, avoiding the need to work past retirement age, or funding a dream vacation in Japan, investing requires a deep understanding of the principles of finance as well as those of self-discipline, patience, and sound judgement, free from any emotion or prejudice. While this may feel intimidating at first glance, investing can be extremely manageable with the right guidance and strategies that minimize risks while maximizing returns. By staying informed and educated on the basics of investing, we'll have you on the road to financial success.

Whilst this series masquerades as a comprehensive set of educational guides to the various inroads of investing, it is in fact a chronology of what I have learnt over the years - and from almost every aspect of investing there is. Growing up in a family that had relatively few financial resources, I was always driven to make something of myself and ensure the future security of my loved ones. One of the ways I set out to do this was by ambitiously aiming to make a million dollars in cold hard cash - which seems almost comical when I look back on it now as I had no idea why I chose this figure! A million dollars was just an arbitrary number that I decided upon when I didn't fully comprehend what it meant, or how life-changing it could be. I just thought to myself "I think having a sum of money would really help my family along", so, with this goal in mind, I began researching and investing in various different fields; from stocks to bonds to real estate to swing trading, and so on! My journey has been far from easy, but every step along the way has been incredibly rewarding as I've continued to learn about investing and building my wealth. Now, whilst making money is still a priority/hobby for me, having time with my family is what really matters - and is ultimately more satisfying than reaching any arbitrary figure.

Once I had achieved my goal of amassing a million dollars, it was not that such an amount was not enough; on the contrary, it is certainly a significant sum, and having so much money at once gave me a feeling of great accomplishment. However, I found that I didn't want to stop there. It wasn't just about wanting to make more money; it was about wanting to keep on experiencing the joy and sense of fulfilment from investing. As a youth, I had the dream of being rich and financially free, but with more experience, I now invest because I've learnt to love it! After sixteen years of engaging in this activity, I had finally come up with a system which enabled me to make consistent wins with most forms of investing. So, I figured, why should I let this newfound understanding go to waste? Why should I stop now when things were going so well?

When I decided to start learning about investing, I made sure that I was as prepared and organized as possible. I researched thoroughly, making notes on who offered the best services, the cheapest rates, and which brokerages had a reputation for being trustworthy. As someone who is naturally meticulous, it only made sense to take an in-depth approach to this as well. So, I made sticky notes, wrote in journals, and took copious notes in Word documents - all with the intention of compiling my thoughts throughout the process. Fast forward sixteen years later and here I am writing a series of books based on my experiences!

To ensure accuracy when writing this series from different perspectives - such as in 'Investing for Women' - I asked friends and fellow investors for their input to add further insight into each book. In fact, much of what is written regarding investing has been pre-written by me over time in various forms - be it a scribbled note or a more detailed outline of what I personally needed to know to invest in that field. Although not an expert in all areas of investment, through years of research and experience (and help from others!) I have been able to piece together content that reflects a diverse range of perspectives within this field.

Overall, this series of books is an amalgamation of much of my own research and experiences - some of which I have been continuing the entire time – others of which I've found either not profitable, or only mildly profitable, and so I've ditched them in favour of the better-earning ones! I have also included the thoughts, opinions and input from others involved in the investing world, to ensure accurate representation from a variety of perspectives. It has been a fun journey putting together all the pieces and rewarding at the same time. I am excited to share my knowledge and insight into investing with you all.

This series of handbooks provides a comprehensive guide for even the most beginner investor who is looking to start investing with confidence and ease. Each book dives deep into different aspects of investing, providing readers with the essential knowledge and information they need to make smart decisions when it comes to managing their money. These books are tailored specifically for those who want to gain a better understanding of investing in the financial markets and successfully managing their portfolios over time. Despite my American-based viewpoint, anyone can follow the principles explained within these pages regardless of their country. By reading this series from beginning to end, readers will be equipped with all the key tools necessary for success in investing and achieving long-term financial independence.

In addition to straightforward advice on how to invest, this series also offers guidance on everything from basic stock market terminology to more complex financial instruments. Readers will learn about diversification, risk management strategies, cost/benefit analysis, taxes related to investments, and more – giving them a strong foundation of knowledge that can be applied no matter what type of investment they choose.

My goal is for readers not only to understand what's going on in the markets but also to gain insight into why certain strategies have been useful for me, and how you can find the ones that suit you best.

Note:

I'm often asked what investments I'm presently making and it's an important question for those who are seeking to find financial freedom. After giving the matter a great deal of thought, I felt writing this information down in a book would quickly become outdated since I tend to rebalance my investments at least every three months. To provide readers with more up-to-date information, I decided to create a website which will help them understand what I am doing and encourage them to do the same. This website will not only provides details of the investments but also includes facts and figures that illustrate how these strategies can help people achieve their financial objectives. It will offer guidance on how to make wise investment choices and gives insight into the kinds of risk associated with each decision. Furthermore, this website contains detailed advice on how to maximize returns by diversifying your portfolio across multiple asset classes, mitigating losses through careful analysis of market trends, as well as other long-term strategies for achieving financial independence. By taking advantage of all the knowledge provided on this site, readers can feel confident that they have taken steps towards attaining their own financial freedom.

The journey to uncovering the secrets of successful investing can seem daunting, but I'm determined to make it easier for you! By subscribing to my email list, you'll stay up-to-date with the latest books in the series, and eventually be the first to know about my unique investment system. By being on the e-mail list I will also let you know when the website is launched too – exciting! I am constantly thinking "I wish I'd had this when I started! I'd have saved a decade worth of time!"

So, no matter your level of financial literacy, I have comprehensive information for anyone who is keen on learning more. With an array of resources at my disposal, I can give you an in-depth look at the foundation of successful investing. Through these materials, I will provide a thorough look into elements such as risk management principles and best practices, financial forecasting, budgeting techniques, and so much more.

On top of this knowledge base, subscribers will also be given access to exclusive tools such as calculators and other interactive features that can help simplify complex topics like portfolio construction. This way, no matter what your individual goals are when it comes to building wealth through investments - I'm here to help!

By joining my email list you'll have access to all these resources and more. So come on board for this exciting adventure and discover how you can get started investing for success today!

So, with no further ado, let's dive in!

Your Free Bonus Gifts

Accelerate Your Learning

Maximize Your Earning

We are here to help you crush it – no bones about it. To make the most of this book, there are two things you'll need:

1. **FREE RESOURCES**

    We have created a number of free resources for you to take advantage of. Use them to accelerate your learning and maximize your earning!

2. **FURTHER RESOURCES**

    We are constantly striving to continue supporting both our team and our students. We are busy creating a website to better highlight all of our investing tips, tricks and current holdings to help our users better see what we're actually up to! To find out when we launch this, and be alerted when we release other titles, just subscribe to our e-mail list and you'll be the first to know!

THE DAY YOU PLANT THE SEED IS NOT THE DAY YOU EAT THE FRUIT

— FABIENNE FREDRICKSON

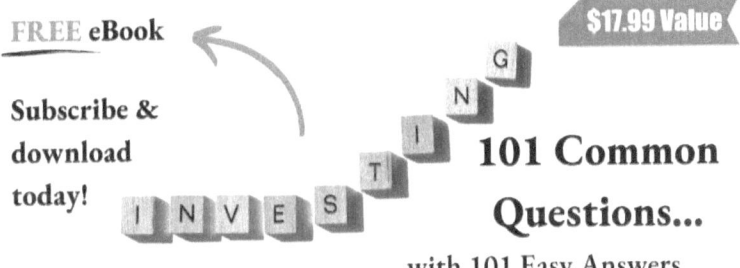

FREE eBook

Subscribe & download today!

$17.99 Value

101 Common Questions...

with 101 Easy Answers

PERSONAL FINANCE

MANAGE YOUR MONEY BETTER

FREE eBook

Subscribe & download today!

$17.99 Value

Subscribe To The Newsletter and Join Us!

- Find out the secrets to investing safely
- Join the growing FIRE (Financially Independent Retire Early) Movement!
- Live your passive income lifestyle...

www.thefirefund.com/free-gift

Table of Contents

Foreword to the Series _____ vii
Your Free Bonus Gifts _____ xiii
Introduction _____ 7
Chapter 1: Stock _____ 9
    A Brief History of the Stock Market _____ 10
    Types of Stocks _____ 14
    Why Companies Issue Shares _____ 16
    Why Own a Stock? _____ 17
    Buying and Selling Stocks _____ 18
    Stock Tickers, Metrics, and Tables _____ 19
    What Is a Stock Exchange? _____ 20
    How Share Prices Are Set _____ 21
    Stock Market Supply and Demand _____ 21
    Matching Buyers to Sellers _____ 22
    Key Takeaways _____ 23
Chapter 2: Variations _____ 24
    Bonds _____ 25

Exchange Traded Funds (ETFs) _____ 26

Mutual Funds _____ 28

Real Estate Investment Trusts (REITs) _____ 31

Index Funds _____ 33

Key Takeaways _____ 34

Chapter 3: How to Analyze a Stock _____ 36

Fundamental Analysis _____ 37

Financial Statements _____ 38

Financial Ratio _____ 39

Technical Analysis _____ 40

Understanding Indicators for Technical Analysis _____ 41

How to do Technical Analysis _____ 42

Underlying Assumptions _____ 43

Technical vs. Fundamental Analysis _____ 45

Limitations of Technical Analysis _____ 46

Key Takeaways _____ 47

Chapter 4: Economic Factors to Consider _____ 48

Economic Trends Investors Should Watch _____ 49

Key Takeaways _____ 56

Chapter 5: Investment Strategies _____ 58

Picking the Right Stocks _____ 58

The Best Time of the Day to Buy Stocks _____ 60

Methods to Raise Capital as an Investor _____ 61

Gilts _____ 63

Overseas Shares _____ 65

Short Selling — 67
Options Trading — 69
Penny Stocks — 71
Value Investing — 73
Growth Investing — 75
Dollar Cost Averaging — 76
Bear Market vs. Bull Market — 77
Key Takeaways — 79

Chapter 6: Value Investing — 80

What Is Value Investing? — 80
What Makes a Great Stock? — 82
Intrinsic Value and Value Investment — 83
Determining Intrinsic Value With the Price-to-Book Ratio — 83
Markets Are Not Efficient — 84
Do Not Follow the Herd — 84
Value Investing Requires Diligence — 85
Why Do Stocks Become Undervalued? — 85
Avoid Value Traps — 86
Value Investing Strategies — 87
Couch Potato Investment — 88
The Risk of Value Investing — 88
Benjamin Graham Case Study — 89
Warren Buffett Case Study — 89
Key Takeaways — 90

Chapter 7: Growth Investing — 91

What Is Growth Investing? _____ 92

Understanding Growth Investing _____ 92

Popular Types of Growth Investment _____ 93

What to Look for in Growth Investing _____ 94

Evaluating a Company's Potential for Growth _____ 96

Strong Historical Earnings Growth _____ 97

Strong Forward Earnings Growth _____ 97

Strong Profit Margins _____ 98

Strong Return on Equity _____ 98

A Step-By-Step Guide to Getting Started _____ 98

Growth Investing vs. Value Investing _____ 101

Key takeaways _____ 101

Chapter 8: Day Trading _____ 103

The Basics of Day Trading _____ 103

Why Day Trading Is Controversial _____ 104

How Does a Day Trader Get Started? _____ 105

Day Trading Strategies _____ 108

Risks of Day Trading _____ 110

What Makes Day Trading Difficult? _____ 111

Day Trading Examples _____ 112

Key Takeaways _____ 113

Chapter 9: Swing Trading _____ 114

What Is Swing Trading? _____ 114

Understanding Swing Trading _____ 115

Advantages of Swing Trading _____ 115

Pros and Cons ___117

Day Trading vs. Swing Trading ___118

Swing Trading Tactics ___119

Real-World Example ___120

Key Takeaways ___121

Chapter 10: Your Stock Portfolio ___123

What Is Stock Correlation? ___124

Positive vs. Negative Stock Correlation ___124

The Correlation Coefficient ___125

How to Calculate Stock Correlation ___126

Why Stock Correlation Matters for Investors ___127

Making Uncorrelated Assets Correlated ___128

Using Correlation for Your Portfolio ___129

Key Takeaway ___133

Chapter 11: Tax Planning ___134

Investment Taxes ___135

Reduced Tax Burden ___135

Tax on Dividends ___137

Tax on Interest ___138

Tax on Capital Gains ___139

Tax Losses and Wash Sales ___141

Hold the Shares Inside an IRA, 401(k), or Other Tax-Advantaged Account ___142

Key Takeaways ___142

Chapter 12: Strategies for Mitigating Risk ___144

    Key Takeaways _____ 148

Chapter 13: Money Management _____ 150

    What Does the Term Money Management Imply? _____ 151

    The Importance of Money Management _____ 151

    Principles of Money Management _____ 152

    Key Takeaways _____ 154

Chapter 14: Cash Flow _____ 156

    What Is Cash Flow? _____ 156

    Categories of Cash Flow _____ 157

    Importance of Cash Flow From Investing _____ 158

    Key Takeaways _____ 158

Conclusion _____ 160

Glossary _____ 163

References _____ 165

Introduction

Your money mindset can be likened to a parachute while you are skydiving. It can either save you or it can cost you your life.

–David Angway

To invest is to generate returns from an asset over a specific period of time. However, it's not guaranteed that you will always make a profit as an investor. Chances are that the odds will be stacked against you. But the degree of risk you'll be exposed to depends on how much return you expect on your investments, how quickly you want to make profits, and your wealth of relevant information.

The truth is that, in many cases, new investors venture into the finance world with little or no knowledge of what a good investment entail. Given that much-unfiltered information is accessible online, it is easy to fall victim to falsehoods, which could render your efforts futile. As a beginner, it's normal to be clueless about the nuance of investment. Like any skill, there is a starting point and room to improve. You should, however, be willing to learn and act with discipline.

It's essential to know how stocks, among other securities, work to excel as an investor. It is also crucial to understand how each security can be effectively analyzed since they have different characteristics. Individuals with inadequate knowledge of how to grow and manage their finances may have a hard time creating an efficient stock portfolio, but this book will simplify what investing is. You'll be introduced to the different mediums through which stocks can be picked. If you struggle with understanding indicators like the famed candlestick chart, this book will demystify this tool and finally make it accessible to you. The open-trade market is typically volatile, and this book will guide you to benefit from its highs and be protected from its dreaded lows. After all, timing is everything for an investor.

> Individuals with inadequate knowledge of how to grow and manage their finances may have a hard time creating an efficient stock portfolio, but this book will simplify what investing is.

Variety is a necessary factor that determines how far an investor can aim. In this book, you will discover how to create a well-diversified and successful portfolio, even as a beginner. Take advantage of the pro tips at the end of every chapter and prepare to be launched to greater heights as a stock investor.

Chapter 1

Stock

I will tell you how to become rich. Close the doors, be fearful when others get greedy; be greedy when others become fearful.

–Warren Buffett

Before I decided to seek knowledge that would help me make the most out of investments, the only place I came across stock trading was on the television while enjoying the business news. I would eventually understand that stocks were representations of an individual's ownership of shares in a company. It seemed as though investors purchased stocks because they hoped they would appreciate over time.

While that is the basic interpretation of stock, from an expert's standpoint, the stock is defined as an investment security that represents the fractional ownership of a corporation—you are purchasing what is called "shares." Automatically, this makes you a shareholder in the company because you have become entitled to a fraction of the company's profits.

A Brief History of the Stock Market

The stock market's history dates back centuries, with the first known stock exchange established in Antwerp, Belgium, in the 16th century. Before that, many markets had similar characteristics to the "stock markets." For instance, a system once existed where "courtiers de change" took care of debts related to the agricultural industry throughout France (Hur, 2018). This is widely believed to be the first significant brokerage where debt exchange was carried out. Years later, bankers in Verona, Genoa, Florence, and other parts of Italy started trading government securities (Kikorangii, 2021).

Antwerp was the home of a very influential family called the Van der Beurze family; therefore, stock exchanges were called Beurzen. The presence of these exchanges also made the city the commercial capital of Belgium. Though these early institutions had many similarities with modern stock markets, they never traded actual stocks pertaining to the shares of a company. They sold other forms of securities, such as personal debt, business debt, and government affairs. Hence, while the organizations and overall structure were similar, the exchanged items differed.

Trading the Shares of a Public Company

Several years later, the first publicly traded company came into existence: the East India Company. It happened that, in those days, it was too risky for a single company to sail across the oceans, as many of the voyages were attacked by pirates or never made it home for several other reasons. Investors were wary of this and decided to find a way to reduce their risk exposure. The result was a company created in 1600 called "Governor and Company of Merchants of London Trading with the East Indies." This was the famous East India Company, and it was the first company to use a limited liability formula (Hur, 2018). Investors quickly realized that investing in multiple voyages was preferable to investing in a single voyage and risking losing everything if the ship failed to deliver. The concept was so successful that other charters in countries all over the world began to follow suit.

The Dutch East India Company officially issued shares on the Amsterdam exchange. These shares were sold in 1602 to investors, who were then entitled to a certain percentage of the company, depending on how many shares they owned.

In the early days, stock exchanges were often informal gatherings where buyers and sellers would meet to trade securities. These exchanges were usually in coffee shops or public places (Smigel, 2022). There was very little regulation regarding stock market activities during this era, and few people understood its significance. As time passed, it became more challenging to distinguish illegitimate businesses from real ones; many companies ceased the payment of dividends periodically received by their shareholders. Eventually, the government of England banned the issuance of shares in 1825.

The First Modern Stock Market

As the stock market grew in popularity and importance, formalized exchanges were established. The New York Stock

Exchange (NYSE) is arguably the biggest and most famous of its kind. It was founded in 1817 and is located in New York City. Although the London Stock Exchange had been around since 1801, it couldn't achieve its true potential due to the ban on the issuance of shares in England; thus, the New York Exchange quickly cemented its place as the number one exchange in the world.

The stock market has evolved significantly over time and has become an essential component of the global financial system. In the nineteenth and twentieth centuries, numerous more stock exchanges arose in other nations; nowadays, every country has its own stock market, and there are several important ones, including the well-known New York Exchange.

Over the years, the stock market has also witnessed considerable technical advances. Stock ticker devices were launched in the early twentieth century, allowing investors to follow the price of stocks in real time. Electronic trading has become the standard with the advancement of computers and the internet, with most deals completed electronically.

Many markets have collapsed, and financial crises have occurred, but the stock market has always rebounded and continued to thrive. Today, the stock market is an essential aspect of the global economy, playing an important role in the financial well-being of individuals, corporations, and governments worldwide.

In recent years, the stock market has grown increasingly international, with investors from all over the world able to trade assets on multiple exchanges. The globalization of the stock market has been greatly aided by technological and communication improvements, as well as the deregulation of financial markets in many nations (Hur, 2018).

There have been many individuals who have played significant roles in the development of the stock market. Some of the key figures in the history of the stock market include:

- **William Hoxton**: William Hoxton is credited with establishing the first stock exchange in Antwerp, Belgium, in the 16th century.

- **Edward Smith**: Edward Smith established the first stock exchange in London in the 17th century.

- **Alexander Hamilton**: Alexander Hamilton played a crucial role in developing the NYSE. He supported the establishment of the NYSE and worked to create a stable financial system in the United States.

- **Charles Dow**: Charles Dow, along with Edward Jones, founded Dow Jones & Company and created the Dow Jones Industrial Average (DJIA), one of the most widely followed stock market indices in the world.

- **Benjamin Graham**: Benjamin Graham improved security analysis and postulated many widely accepted investment principles.

- **Warren Buffett**: Warren Buffett is one of the most successful investors in history and is known for his value investing approach. He is the chairman and CEO of Berkshire Hathaway, a holding company that owns a diverse portfolio of businesses.

- **John Bogle**: John Bogle is the founder of Vanguard Group, a mutual fund company that popularized the concept of index funds. He is also known for his advocacy of low-cost investing and criticism of the mutual fund industry.

Types of Stocks

Fundamentally, there are numerous types of stocks, with their differences being categorized by distinctive factors like dividends and voting rights. The types of stocks include:

- **Common stocks**: Investors make purchases of common stocks in public companies. This means they have become shareholders as they own some percentage of the company. Common stock owners may be paid in dividends, but they are not often guaranteed, nor are they fixed. The level of their ownership in the company is proportional to their voting rights.

- **Preferred stocks**: Unlike common stocks, where dividends aren't guaranteed, preferred stocks pay fixed dividends. This helps stock owners to be able to evaluate and have expectations of a certain amount of income every year. Also, they do not have voting rights. In similarity to the common stock, owners get a seat at the table when the company's earnings are being distributed. More importantly, in the event of bankruptcy or liquidation, preferred stock owners remain ahead of common stock owners when the company's assets are distributed.

- **Growth stocks**: Investors who buy growth stocks usually do so for a very reasonable shot at success. It taps into the strong and rising demands of the customers on a long-term basis, primarily when the services or products provided are widely supported and patronized. With growth stocks, the risks are high, but the returns can be very worth it if you make purchases and are willing to take risks. May I add that competition is quite fierce in the growth stock market, and in the worst-case scenario, when the stock is disrupted, it can suffer a quick decline in value.

- **Value investing stocks**: Individual investors who make value stocks a part of their portfolios are perceived as being conservative. This is because it is an investment heavily influenced by popular corporations that have peaked in their businesses and can no longer create any further expansion. These companies, over time, have overcome every business barrier there ever was. Therefore, they have become more mature and can be relied on in terms of price stability and positive exposure to stocks.

- **Income stocks**: Income stocks are also known as dividend stocks. This means that the financial gains derived from stocks are presented as dividends. Like value-investing stocks, income-producing stocks are mature and conservative but have a shorter duration for a long-term growth opportunity. I would recommend the purchase of income stocks for individual investors (older people nearing or already retired) who may have an immediate need for the cash in their portfolios.

Why Companies Issue Shares

Generally, registered companies or corporations are excellent structures for any business to raise capital. Some reasons why corporations sell shares include:

- **Expansion of funding**: Some start-ups or companies that are in their developmental stage and are looking to expand may issue shares to investors. Companies in their early stages might have a low turnover rate. Therefore, they have to bank on issuing shares to provide equity.

- **Maximize wealth**: Another specific reason for the issuance of shares is for companies to build and maximize wealth. Take a look at it from the investor's point of view. You buy shares in companies that are small and private for the primary purpose of generating wealth that is accumulated through your investment earnings. This can only be guaranteed after you have studied the company's goals, strategies, and focus that drive them to accomplishment. You may feel inclined to invest a considerable sum of money to help you become a part of the company's decision-making.

- **Avoid debt**: Issuing shares helps companies avoid the possibility of going into debt. On the flip side, issuing stocks can aid in the future facilitation of loans. When these investors make purchases of shares in these companies, it automatically improves their financial stability. It would be easy to borrow because there is a guarantee that they have the means to make a refund.

- **Listing shares**: Is the term "listing" familiar to you in the finance world as a beginner investor? When issuing stocks, the listing represents the shares on the list where stocks are being traded. To better understand how a listing works, every stock exchange has its own list that contains rules and essential requirements that include past financial statements, amongst others.

- **Raising capital**: Companies issue shares to raise money to offset start-up costs. Building a corporation can be financially demanding, with costs like rent, attorney fees, equipment and furniture purchases, insurance, and security deposits, among other vital expenses. These can be figured out early by issuing shares to ordinary individuals who want to make investments.

Why Own a Stock?

Typically, the closest thing to an answer that you would get after asking yourself this question is the potential of your capital's appreciation over time. Investors who prefer to hold on to stocks for an extended period often become rewarded with excellent returns. Nonetheless, you should make peace with the fact that just as the price of stocks can rise, they can also decline in the open market. The benefits of owning stock are numerous, and the pros outweigh the cons as long as you keep in the back of your mind that the market is usually volatile, and profit is not always guaranteed.

> Nonetheless, you should make peace with the fact that just as the price of stocks can rise, they can also decline in the open market.

With stock investments, you will stay ahead of inflation, accumulate wealth, be prepared for retirement, and save on taxes. Being a part of the stock market requires that if you are not pleased with the kind of management operated by the corporation you invested in, you are allowed to sell your stocks. But if the arrangement pleases or resonates with you, you can hold on to your stocks for a long period and hope that it produces favorable returns.

Buying and Selling Stocks

Do you wonder how you can buy and sell stocks efficiently to produce good returns despite the market's volatility? Initially, I was not entirely sure how stocks were bought, whether they were physical, or I had to sit with several business people over a round table to make purchases. Eventually, I realized that I had a lot to learn about how the market truly works. To buy stocks, you will require the aid of a stockbroker. The stockbroker can be a human or an online platform that serves the same purpose since these stocks cannot be bought directly. The most important thing required of you by the online stockbroker is to select what kind of investment you would like to make and decide how the trade should be conducted. For a physical stockbroker, it is a similar process, except that you have the help of an actual human being who can make the trade on your behalf, depending on your type of investment.

Stocks can be bought on licensed exchange platforms, where they are listed to be purchased or sold by investors. The exchange is done between the buyer and the seller, with the stockbroker acting as an intermediary that facilitates the success of the trade. There are two major exchange markets in the United States: NASDAQ, established in the early 70s, and the New York Stock Exchange (NYSE), founded way back in the 1800s. For a beginner investor, the easiest way to buy and sell stocks is to open an online brokerage account, fund it, and place an order to buy stocks. Although this may seem like the most straightforward way, it is not necessarily the wisest choice. This is because it requires brief research on the platform and the kind of investment you want to purchase or with whom you want to exchange it.

Stock Tickers, Metrics, and Tables

Like every other avenue for maximizing wealth, there are conventions, metrics, and rules that oversee how trades are executed and documented. Every investor, whether a beginner or an expert, requires the aid of charts, stock tables, and metrics, amongst others, to understand how the market functions. These charts and tables will help you successfully read and understand what transpires on the daily trades and how you can place orders with an available stockbroker.

In the United States, key indexes are utilized as an economic indicator that measures the present conditions of the stock market to predict future trends. The purpose of these economic indicators is to capture the status of a sector in the stock market from one moment to the next. With these indexes, you can study them to tell whether the market is up (on the rise) or down (declining).

Ideally, any individual investor should spend quality time developing clean and easy-to-read tables, workspaces, and charts that can help develop the ability to interpret market activity. However, various financial websites offer numerous chart options for stocks and other types of investments where you can easily access stock charts. You do not need to create your own charts to analyze stocks, although professionals and investment experts work with the ones they make. It can be time-consuming but very much worth the effort if you try to set one up. It comes in handy when the market gets competitive, and you need to make smart trade decisions quickly. An already-setup chart can help you become a more efficient and promising trader.

What Is a Stock Exchange?

Imagine for a moment that you went to a big open market,

maybe a trade fair. There are lots of stalls and people from every part of the state convening to make trades by exchanging funds for items they would love to have. A stock exchange can perform a similar function as the imagined trade fair. It allows people to connect and buy or sell stocks, equities, bonds, and other financial commodities. Trading stocks often requires the presence of a stockbroker to be successful. You must also understand the existing connection or relationship between exchanges and the corporations that trade them.

How Share Prices Are Set

The prices that shares go by are determined by different factors, as they could serve as a pointer to how long investments in their entirety can benefit you, even in retirement. To bolster this opinion, it means that over time, the price of a share will be determined by its earning power. The better a company does, the better the chances of favorable prices. Therefore, once a corporation decides to become part of the stock market, where its shares are now made public to be bought or sold, its price is solely determined by the demand and supply rates.

Technically, it is impossible to predict how well a stock will do or when it will, but the share price movement can be monitored to understand how it works.

Stock Market Supply and Demand

In economics, the laws guiding demand and supply are a theory that explains the connection between the availability (supply) of a product and the desire (demand) for it. Logically, understanding this connection has provided me with good insight into the economic factors that determine the price of a stock or at least influence it. In the course of my process as a beginner, I would realize that the low availability of a stock or any item generally and a high demand for it in the economy automatically boost its price. Then, when an item is highly available when there is a low demand for it, the price suffers a decline.

The influence of this economic law on stocks and other securities cannot be underestimated. The individual stocks that make up the stock market have their prices determined by how much a company's product is available or desired in the economy.

Matching Buyers to Sellers

The only thing a buyer and a seller have in common should be a market. And so far, you may have figured out that for that to be effective, there is a need for a broker. The broker's function in this regard is to understand the needs of each party, bring them together for negotiation, and oversee the trading process between the individuals.

On online stock exchange platforms, the process is facilitated by market makers or specialists, and it entails matching the orders of two opposite parties who want to buy the same quantity of a specific security and another who has the same amount to sell. This way, the correspondents with similar price ranges within proximity become paired, and a transaction is affected.

Key Takeaways

- A stock is a fraction of a company that, when sold to individuals, makes them shareholders and entitles them to a part of that company's profits.

- To trade stocks on the market, you need the services of a broker.

- Tickers, charts, and tables all reflect an investor's confidence and can be strong indicators of how well or how badly an economy is doing.

- In the financial market, supply and demand are significant determinants of the price of stocks and other types of securities.

- In the last decade, matching buyers and sellers has evolved to become almost completely automated and computerized.

- Investing is a long-term approach in the market to building wealth, while trading requires short-term techniques to maximize frequent returns.

Investments come in different variants, and the next chapter will provide insight into the available options and what they entail.

Chapter 2

Variations

You must know what you own and know why you own it.

–Peter Lynch

Investments are not limited to stocks; they come in variations, and they can be used as a metric to determine whether the expected return on investment is worth the risks or volatility that it might be subjected to over the long haul. Also, variations in the finance world can illustrate the measurement of the investment returns securities have to offer and how they can differ.

> Variations in the finance world can illustrate the measurement of the investment returns securities have to offer and how they can differ.

This chapter highlights the other types of securities, their benefits, and their downsides.

Bonds

In finance, bonds can be described as an investment security. It is in the form of a loan given to investors, who might be corporations, municipalities, states, or independent governing bodies that seek to fund projects like road construction and erect new infrastructure. Similarly, corporations have urgent needs or will often need to fund specific aspects like building new office compartments, undertaking projects that will yield good returns, and hiring employees, amongst other operations that require financing. Most times, the amount of funds these corporations or municipalities require is large, and banks cannot offer them. This is why they resort to buying bonds instead of stocks. While the borrowers of bonds are called issuers, the owners are called creditors or debt holders.

The details of issuing a bond usually include the date (also known as the maturity day) when the bond issue payment is due. The interest payment is either fixed or can vary. The borrower initiates it. Thus, an issuer is expected to pay back by the stipulated time. As an individual bond investor, you can give out these loans to big organizations with interest rates that serve as your profit. You are also allowed to make purchases of new bonds from other investors after you have lent some to issuers and they have been able to raise capital for their projects.

Bonds, like stocks, can be said to be one of the most familiar investment securities. When an issuer returns the principal amount of the loan borrowed, and the investor has generated returns, the interest rate is known as the "coupon rate." You must also understand that the market prices for bonds are determined by their attributes. Some of these bonds are:

- Puttable bonds
- Zero-coupon bonds
- Convertible bonds

All of these bonds vary in characteristics as well as in prices daily. Thus, similar to stocks and other equities, the laws of demand and supply easily influence it.

In conclusion, bonds are a good investment and, compared to stocks, are less volatile. Bonds can be purchased with the aid of brokers who are specialized in that regard.

Exchange Traded Funds (ETFs)

An ETF, as its name implies, can be traded on an exchange market just like stocks and other investments. It can be described as a type of fund and marketable security that can be easily purchased and sold on the market because of the price of its shares. The fund usually holds multiple assets in place. It can contain hundreds and thousands of stocks across numerous enterprises. You can also choose to segregate the fund by sector.

ETFs can be structured to perform the function of a tracker over a sector, index, commodity, asset, or even the price of an individual asset in a more extensive range of diversified portfolios. There are various types of ETFs available to investors to serve as an income speculating technique, to generate income, and to offset risk in any portfolio. Some of the types of ETFs include:

- Passive and active ETFs
- Bond ETFs
- Commodity ETFs
- Inverse ETFs
- Currency ETFs
- Stock ETFs
- Sector/Industry ETFs
- Leveraged ETFs

All of these types of ETFs are available on the market if you ever consider using ETFs as a form of building a diversified portfolio. Investing in the fund is presumably easy as long as you can follow the steps outlined below:

- Find an investing platform.
- Do extensive research work on ETFs.
- Consider a trading strategy. I would recommend that you spread out your investment costs over a period as a good strategy for a beginner investor.

The satisfying part of investing in ETFs is the fact that they can be traded through online brokers as well as through traditionally specialized brokers. Whether you settle for the online investing process or the traditional one, after creating the account, it has to be funded before an investment process can kick off; your broker will be the one to determine what funding method is suitable for your brokerage account. After that stage has been completed, apply the same measure that is used in the purchase of shares of stock when buying and selling an ETF.

ETFs have their benefits. They do not require high costs to manage. The expenses are low because they majorly perform tracking indexes and assets. Frequently, brokers offer no-commission trading for ETFs that do not cost much. As a beginner investor, this puts you at an advantage as it reduces your costs. Another benefit is your access to many stocks and the ability to manage the risks involved with each security through diversification.

Mutual Funds

The concept of mutual funds is almost similar to that of ETFs. It serves as a vehicle that puts together all kinds of investment securities for individual investors or shareholders. The essence of a mutual fund is to make provisions for an avenue to generate capital rewards. Indeed, individuals or beginners become investors because they want to maximize and accumulate wealth. Mutual funds allow for that, as they are structured to meet those personal investment objectives that you have. In most cases, mutual fund portfolios are managed by professional money managers who, through their skills and experience, can help you allocate your fund assets so that you can generate interest.

Like other funds, mutual funds allow individuals, whether beginner investors or experienced professionals, to create a diversified portfolio that can include other securities like bonds, stocks, and equities, amongst others. The bottom line is that you require the aid of a professional money manager to run this fund successfully and effectively. In the United States of America, most mutual funds are associated with giant investment corporations like Oppenheimer, Vanguard, Fidelity Investments, etc. You must know that despite the experience and reputation of these large corporations, their mutual funds are being managed by a professional who is legally certified to meet the unique needs of these investors.

In any trading market, you can only derive the value of the securities in your mutual fund portfolio through an estimation of the value each security possesses. I would say that buying a share in a mutual fund is synonymous with purchasing its performance if it is in the portfolio. This is because each security making up the mutual fund portfolio has to have a good market performance for its value to be determined. One distinctive feature of this fund is that, unlike stocks, where individual investors get to partake in the voting processes of the company, mutual funds are not accorded that benefit. The shareholders do not possess voting rights of any kind.

The types of mutual funds include:

- Stock funds

- Index funds
- Bond funds
- Balanced funds
- Money market funds
- Income funds

These categories of funds, like the ETFs, have similarities just as much as you could highlight their differences; both funds employ consistent strategies to aid the diversification of an investment portfolio. The prices for the mutual fund on the trading market are deduced by dividing the total value of the diverse securities present in the portfolio by the aggregate of the outstanding shares (for better comprehension, outstanding shares are usually in possession of shareholders, institutional investors, and so on). A practical of how mutual funds work is:

Assume that, as a beginner investor, you purchase Microsoft stock. Of course, you know that you are buying a part of the company—this makes you a shareholder with partial ownership benefits. There are specific ways to make proceeds on a quarterly or annual basis with that decision. The shares that you have purchased from Microsoft may appreciate over time, which will provide you with the opportunity to sell them for a profit. Moreover, you will be granted the choice of either receiving a check for the distribution of the funds or making new share purchases by reinvesting those profits. I would also recommend it to beginner investors because you get the support of a full-time manager who uses stealth research and trading skills to monitor and manage your portfolio effectively. They are usually quite affordable.

Real Estate Investment Trusts (REITs)

Simply defined, real estate investment trusts are corporations that own and operate real estate or similar assets to generate greater profits. You may have become familiar with REITs at some point. These trusts invest in residential and commercial buildings like malls, warehouses, hotels, resorts, loans, etc. You may also be aware that in most real estate processes, investors acquire these properties to resell them to make profits. With REITs, the opposite is true. You do not buy the properties to resell them. Instead, these properties are developed to be utilized as a part of an investment portfolio.

One of the questions on your mind is probably why REITs would be a good investment for you. One reason is that they're veritable avenues for individual investors, even beginners, to own a share of the profits made by these organizations without purchasing properties. Like other securities like stocks and bonds, REITs are traded openly on the exchange market. Some REITs are registered with the SEC but not showcased publicly on the exchange market to be bought or sold. They are called non-traded REITs.

Real estate is lucrative and can be very beneficial to your investment portfolio, but it could be detrimental to ignore the fact that it has its risks. Some of the benefits involved are stable cash flow through dividends, the risk-adjusted returns are attractive, and it can be a reasonable means of diversification in your portfolio. These risks are:

- Low growth.

- Managing publicly traded REITs may cost a lot to handle them efficiently, and it doesn't change the fact that they are subject to market risks.

- Difficulty in the prediction of the value of non-traded REITs because the publicly traded REITs have their share value transparent and readily accessible.

- Non-traded REITs do not have internal employees like other investment companies. Instead, it is run by an external manager. This can result in strained situations where shareholders develop a conflict of interest if the incentives involved do not align with their interests.

- They lack liquidity because if you ever find yourself in a crisis where you need to sell an asset to raise money urgently, it might be challenging to achieve that with non-traded REITs.

If you are hoping to avoid the risks involved in non-traded REITs, you can invest in publicly traded REITs—they are readily accessible on the exchange market and can be purchased with the aid of a broker-dealer. REITs, ETFs, and mutual funds afford investors the opportunity to buy shares.

Index Funds

Index funds serve the purpose of tracking the details of a financial market index. As a mutual fund, it provides broad market exposure, meager portfolio turnover, and low operating costs. Index mutual funds are ideal for beginners nearing retirement or who have retired already and possess individual retirement accounts (IRAs) and 401(k)s. These are excellent choices for investments as part of your portfolio, mainly if your objective is to save up for the later years of your life.

The entire idea behind an index mutual fund is that it seeks to mimic the index of the stock market as a whole, helping you decide what security to invest in and being able to deduce the perfect time to buy or sell the shares. All through this process, the index fund monitors and matches its own performances. Its advantages include:

1. Low expense ratios.

2. It generates lower taxes for individual investors.

3. It is the perfect choice for investors who want to "buy and hold."

4. Index funds yield dependable long-term profits.

5. The mutual fund, because of its diversification feature, can help lower risks.

The demerits of index funds are:

1. Although the long-term gains are typically substantial, index funds follow the market and may be affected by the downtrends regularly experienced by the market.

2. They are not intended to be used to "beat" the market but rather to try to match it, minus their typically small expenses.

3. They are inflexible.

Key Takeaways

- Bonds as a unit are tradable assets or securities issued by companies.

- ETFs can contain all investment securities, including stocks, bonds, and other commodities. Some of these stocks are U.S. holdings, while others are international.

- ETFs' share prices, unlike those of mutual funds, fluctuate as they are bought and sold.

- Mutual funds cut across all kinds of investments and function effectively according to their investment goals and the type of capital each security has to obtain.

- REITs can prove to be a source of a steady income stream, but they have very little to offer in terms of capital appreciation.

- Index funds, as a diversified portfolio, are designed to reflect the features and activities of a financial market index.

As a beginner investor, it is vital to research the type of portfolio you want for diversification. The next chapter will expound on the strategic ways to analyze a stock and other measures to consider concerning your investment choice.

Chapter 3

How to Analyze a Stock

The stock market is filled with individuals who know the price of everything but the value of nothing.

–Philip Fisher

Analyzing a stock can be likened to deciding to go shopping for a car. You can easily make a major decision based on the car's technical specs. For example, you might make considerations over its ability to drift, how good the engine is, the revving sound, the reputation of the manufacturer, and whether it is manual or automatic. To attain these speculations, it is essential to consider how the car feels on the road. Does it guarantee a smooth ride, or are there uncertainties? The same analytical technique can be applied to stock research.

Understanding how to evaluate a stock will significantly benefit you as an investor. However, it means that you have to put into consideration a range of factors before making a purchase. This chapter will evaluate in an in-depth manner the analysis of stock fundamentally, how the company's finances can be a strong influence on your decision-making process, and most certainly decide whether the stock deserves a space in your investment portfolio.

Fundamental Analysis

The fundamental analysis of stocks by a beginner should come naturally. The natural feeling of inquisition and curiosity that stems from the urge to have a concrete understanding of a subject matter is something that ensues from within. Most people who developed a genuine interest in painting, law, or architecture, for example, didn't have such passions forced on them. In the same vein, constantly relying on extrinsic motivation to fire up your drive for stock analysis and investment may be, quite likely, futile. The need for it must develop from within you, just like Warren Buffett, who not only invests but also enjoys the process of making investments.

Most times, it is better that you have a personal interest in how things work in the finance world and employ the services of other professionals to perform specific tasks that you could have easily pulled off yourself without any hassle. With a fundamental analysis in place, your credibility is ascertained. The process of the fundamental analysis entails building up your mind to be probing. Once your eyes come in contact with something unfamiliar, you want to evaluate what it is and learn about it. It is vital to develop a mind that processes thoughts like an analyst. Usually, whoever describes themselves as an analyst most likely has a specific field they are an expert in, for example, data analysts, system analysts, financial analysts, and network analysts, amongst others. For you, it is stock.

You must focus on that sector and on selecting companies and corporations that are in the industry, perform in-depth research on them, and evaluate their financial statements and all the other necessary information there is about the company. This vital information can include their customers, competitors, and suppliers. You might even physically go to the company to gain first-hand experience and an understanding of how they function. This is essential to connect the dots, create a comparative analysis, and get the bigger picture before investing. All of these take time because it is a process. As long as you can dedicate quality time to getting work done, you are on the right path.

Financial Statements

External stakeholders assess a company's financial statements to evaluate and understand its business value and business performance. The results of this aid their decision-making process. That is, whether it is a good investment measure or not. Internal stakeholders, on the other hand, use a company's financial statement merely to monitor finances and manage them efficiently.

Every organization, whether small or large, has data or records on every business activity performed in the past, currently, or in projected future performances. These activities are subjected to evaluation when the need arises from internal and external factors. Generally, every financial statement in the United States is centered around accepted accounting principles. The reflectivity of these principles' rests on the creation and maintenance of three major types of financial statements, which are:

- The balance sheet.
- The cash flow.
- The income.

Some techniques distinguish how the analytic process goes in private and public corporations. In contrast to private companies, public companies follow through with the "generally accepted accounting principles" standards in a rigorous and conforming manner. Private companies are much more flexible in their financial statement preparation, so they can choose between accrual and cash account systems of statement preparation.

Financial Ratio

Investors and stock analysts often utilize the ratio analysis measure to assess the past and present finances of an organization. As an individual investor, ratio analysis can also help you tell for sure the performance of a company over time and to make predictions or an estimation of their future performances.

Ratio analysis can be described as a quantitative method of revealing a company's operational efficiency, profitability, and liquidation capacity. It is a vital aspect of fundamental equity analysis. The types of ratio analysis include:

- Profitability ratios
- Solvency ratios
- Market prospect ratios
- Efficiency ratios
- Coverage ratios

In most cases where a ratio analysis is done on a company, the analyst (internal or external) utilizes the data derived to influence long-term decision-making.

How can you apply ratio analysis in preparing a company's financial statement? To derive the correct data, an analyst has to compare multiple figures. The company specifies a single financial ratio and estimates it on a fixed cadence (a repetitive and consistent monthly ratio calculation), although some influencing factors like seasonal and momentary fluctuations in the account balances can impact a ratio calculation. Therefore, it is essential to closely study how the company's deductible ratio changes over time. Are there improvements? Is it falling? Are the changes intentional? Perhaps the company wants to change over time. All of these are factors to consider.

Technical Analysis

Technical analysis is used by investors to find opportunities in the market. It makes use of statistical trends, including volume and price movements. Charles Dow introduced the basis for the theory. Technical analysis tools operate under the assumption that past trading activities can be valuable indicators of the security's price movement when combined with appropriate investing rules.

Analysts who have turned professionals often use technical analysis and other research measures to forecast price movements as long as the security already has a pre-existing trading data set. It is a technique that is a lot more common in the commodities market, where traders are more concerned about the prices of securities on a short-term basis.

Understanding Indicators for Technical Analysis

The indicators for technical analysis across every finance enterprise are pretty distinctive. Technical analysts have formulated an evident pattern to advocate for technical analysis in trading. Be reminded that these indicators serve as a measure to predict a security's price movement in the market.

The indicators for technical analysis are strategic and well-structured. That is, some of them are primarily concentrated on discerning the current market trend. Suffice it to say that they support and contrast in certain areas, while the others are strong determinants of how strong a trend is in the market and the possibilities of it being a continual process.

Analysts have made deductions based on solid and reliable indicators for technical analysis, for example:

- Chart patterns
- Price trends
- Oscillators
- Support and resistance level
- Moving averages
- Volume and momentum indicators

How to do Technical Analysis

Investors can always choose the type of analyst they want to become regarding personal investments in securities like stocks. While an investor who decides to be a fundamental analyst has to consider all the fundamentals and values that make up a stock to analyze it properly, a technical analyst merely seeks to make predictions through the assessments of the stock's previous data on volume and price, respectively.

The following are actionable or practical steps that can guide you to do the gold standard of technical analysis of a stock:

- Choose the right approach and develop a strategy or trading system that resonates with you and your objectives.

- Identify securities as well as you can because not every stock might fit with whatever kind of approach or strategy you decide to opt for. It is crucial to find the one that suits you best.

- There is always a right and suitable trading account that fits every type of security, whether options, common stock, futures, etc. This strategy should offer features that help track the technical indicators that you have carefully selected and, at the same time, reduce costs.

- Every approach requires different strategies, which might be a strong determinant of how much you have to participate or function in the process. Tracking and monitoring trades is an essential strategy for market marker visibility.

- Your strategy might have features that require extra tools to help you maximize performance; do not hesitate to use additional tools or software where necessary.

Underlying Assumptions

I have a personal theory that, generally, every phenomenon in the world, every belief, lifestyle, and piece of information of any kind can be subjected to assumptions—and the finance world is not exempted from this theory. It is essential to distinguish between a belief and a fact.

I have a personal theory that, generally, every phenomenon in the world, every belief, lifestyle, and piece of information of any kind can be subjected to assumptions—and the finance world is not exempted from this theory.

It has been ascertained that there are two significant types of investment security analysis:

1. Fundamental analysis

2. Technical analysis

I should reiterate that the fundamental method of analyzing a company's financial statement is to assess the fair value of its business. Technical analysis, on the other hand, only assumes that the price of a security has displayed all information available to the public. Therefore, it is mainly concerned with deducing a statistical analysis of the security's price movement.

Three general assumptions surround a technical trading analysis:

1. The market accounts for all publicly known information: Every detail, from a company's fundamentals to the factors that distinguish the entire market to the study of the market, already has its price attached to the stock. This means that there has already been a conclusive assumption about the costs. Technical analysts conclusively believe that the economic factors of demand and supply influence price movement.

2. Analysts expect that prices will always exhibit trends, irrespective of the time frame. For example, if a technical analyst has carefully observed that a stock price moves in a particular pattern, they may conclude that it will always move at that rate in the future instead of suddenly changing direction.

3. Repetition of history: Technical analysts strongly opine

    that over time, history will repeat itself—inevitably. This is an assumption fuelled by market psychology, where the price of a stock can be predicted based on the outcome of actions influenced by emotions; it could be fear or excitement in any form. They use a chart pattern to gain insight into the particular feeling that has affected the price of a stock in the past, then believe history will repeat itself in subsequent times.

Technical vs. Fundamental Analysis

These two primary schools of thought about analyzing markets can be contrasted as being at either end of the spectrum. Although they share a similarity in purpose in that they are used as a research method to predict future trends in the prices of stocks.

Technical analysis fundamentally differs from fundamental analysis, despite the few similarities that they share. With this method of analysis, the prices of stock and volume are solely inputted. This means that all the publicly available information on the basics of a stock is factored into the cost; as such, there might not be any essential need to be focused on other alternate possible factors that could impact price performance.

On the other hand, it is acceptable to define fundamental analysis as a technique for evaluating securities by measuring the inherent values of a stock. Fundamental analysts, unlike technical analysts, usually leave no stone unturned. They study every basic piece of information, assess the economy, and try to find correlations between the company's financial condition and how it is being managed. Every possibility and characteristic are carefully considered, for example, the company's expenses, assets, the inflow of money, and liabilities. In place of measuring the value of a stock through all of these characteristics, technical analysts utilize chart patterns and trends that can help them to make predictions on the future performances of the stock.

Limitations of Technical Analysis

Investors who believe that the market is highly predictable and that "history repeats itself" are likely to fail. Studying the price market to analyze its future performance is a counterproductive approach and should be disregarded. A better system for analysts, while not an intuitive one, might be to abandon prediction for determining the price market based on its present, seemingly random performance.

Key Takeaways

- With fundamental analysis, you can quickly identify potentially undervalued stocks and fix price targets.

- The essence of financial statement analysis is for internal and external stakeholders to assess the company's value and business performance.

- Ratio analysis makes a comparison between a company's line-item data to gain insights into its liquidity, solvency, profitability, and efficiency generally.

- Technical analysts strongly suggest that the change in price and past trading activities can indicate the movement of the security's price in the long run.

- As a beginner investor, you must understand why technical analysis serves as a gateway to delve into the psychology of a market and become familiar with profitable opportunities.

Chapter 4

Economic Factors to Consider

Becoming a successful investor in the future should be effortless when you understand and let the market do the work for you.

–Adam Messina

In my years of learning and exploring the stock market, neither I nor any professional investor I'm aware of has been able to reliably and consistently predict the market. It is also almost impossible to get the perfect timing for when the market will take an excellent turn. You have to keep your fingers crossed as long as you have applied the right strategies.

Notwithstanding, it is not a gamble. There are constantly influencing factors and indicators, especially in the economy, that impact the rise and fall of stock prices. This way, you can know what is coming against the market. This chapter will give a thorough and clear insight into what these economic influencing factors are and how you can gear up.

Economic Trends Investors Should Watch

Whether it is convenient or not, certain factors cannot be helped in the finance world, especially when it has to do with the economy. It plays a vital role in the stock market because if the economy is thriving, so is the stock market. And if there is a decline, the stock market suffers the same fate. This is why, in most cases, every industry with investments or shares on the stock market relies on the stability and thriving of the economy to guarantee profits.

That's why in some states in the United States where the economy is booming, the market is most likely competitive. People want to buy and make investments because profitability is guaranteed. As long as the economy keeps expanding, they will keep buying. While this is being established, it would not be ideal to shy away from the other side of the coin, where the stock market can take a deep blow when the economy fails.

The following are economic factors that influence stock prices in the economy, whether positively or negatively:

Interest Rates

This is one of the economic factors that can influence the rise or decline of the stock market. When interest rates are high, it becomes tough to borrow money. For example, if you need capital for a business and decide to take out a loan, but you find out that it demands a 30% rate on the returns, you might have to reconsider taking the loan. Therefore, when an economy hits this point in interest rates, it eats into the company's profit margin. In contrast to this, when interest rates are lower in the advent of a struggling economy, stock prices automatically drop. This way, people or corporations can easily borrow money because the interest rates are feasible, providing a boost to the market.

Gross Domestic Product (GDP)

Gross domestic product is a metric representing the complete services and goods a country produces within its borders. It's indicative of the country's economic size and expresses the standard of living within the country.

When a country has a growing GDP, its economy is considered healthy and prosperous. As such, companies will be more open to increasing their workforce and have the purchasing power to do that. In turn, unemployment reduces, and money trickles down, making consumers more likely to spend. This creates a perpetual cycle that generates more income for the people, thereby growing the economy.

However, when the GDP shrinks, the exact opposite kicks into effect. Businesses are more cautious and will try to remain profitable. This will lead to scaling back expansion and production plans to save costs, as well as reducing the workforce, which puts unemployment on the upswing.

Although the effects of GDP on the economy could influence financial markets, no one can accurately predict the relationship between the growth of a country's GDP—negative or positive—and returns in the bond or stock markets. Of course, there is an affiliation between financial markets and the economy's strength in general. However, the relationship is loose and only becomes evident over extremely long timeframes. If anything, GDP can be considered a lagging indicator at best because it reflects the economy's direction in the past, although reasonably recently.

Investors and economists would rather have a positive, steady GDP growth of 1.5% to 3% each year. This range is deemed healthier for developed economies like the United States. If it were faster, concerns about unfeasible economic bubbles and inflation would be in order. Slower growth, on the other hand, typically triggers concerns that economic standards will decline and stagnate. In the event of a higher GDP, the government and the Central Bank would naturally try to remedy the situation by introducing higher interest rates. This measure will help ground the economy and send a ripple effect across many financial markets.

Unemployment

The rate of unemployment in a country is a measure of its economic well-being. The higher the unemployment rate, the fewer jobs the economy produces for the population. And the longer it continues, the more productivity and purchasing power will wane, thereby influencing the mental and physical well-being of the workforce.

Conversely, when unemployment rates are low, it means the economy is healthy. This reflects on stock market performance because investors are more inclined to purchase shares in thriving companies.

Since unemployment rates indicate an unhealthy or healthy economy, it's not far-fetched that they foreshadow stock prices to some degree. Higher unemployment rates show a decline in demand for the products and services of companies, which leads to declining share prices. Investors prefer stable economies, as they give companies the best shot at profitability. So, when that prerequisite is off the table due to unemployment, they are less likely to invest due to increased risks.

Arguments can be made for securities that deviate from this path, like the S&P 500, which has provided astonishing results over the years. Historically, the equity market has performed significantly worse during low unemployment periods. From the 1950s to date, the S&P 500 has generated an annual return rate of 12% whenever unemployment rose beyond the historical average. Compare that to its yearly return rate of 6% when unemployment numbers fall below the historical average.

Of course, there are several reasons why this happens, such as:

- Market valuations are often at their peak during low unemployment periods. As such, future returns could be muted while more opportunities for corrections and downturns are present.

- When the economy is at its strongest, unemployment rates are often low. However, nothing is stopping higher inflation rates during a healthy economy. This prompts the government to take action, tightening the flow of money to dampen the effects of inflation. As a result, financial markets will shift their positions to brace for slow economic growth, which could trigger lower returns in the market.

Trade Wars

Trade wars happen when a country creates tariffs for goods entering its borders. As a result, other foreign countries fire back by imposing their own tariffs, too, to protect their trade. The longer it continues, the more international trade grinds to a halt.

Usually, the idea behind a trade war is simple: a country tries to protect its economy and industries and reduce unemployment. This might work in the short term, as tariffs on foreign goods make domestic producers seem more appealing to local consumers. As a result, the economy would prosper as the GDP grew. And the more businesses grow, the lower unemployment rates drop.

However, the strategy becomes counterintuitive the longer it continues, as some industries start to wane. As a result, unemployment rates begin to pick up again, and the economy starts leading towards a depression. If all that wasn't enough, inflation is also in the mix from when tariffs made imports costlier to purchase.

As trade wars continue and consumer goods prices increase, exports out of the country become so expensive they are unfeasible to exporters. As a result, the industry starts to suffer, and workers are laid off to consolidate costs and remain competitive. If this fails to work, more cost-cutting strategies will be implemented. In a worst-case scenario, the industry could go out of business.

Inflation

Inflation occurs when the demand for products and services correlates with price increments for those products and services, especially in times of strong economic growth. Inflation increases when demand outpaces supply and causes scarce resources to sell at higher price points.

Inflation becomes sustained when demand and spending trump the creation of products and services, thereby forcing producers to increase the price point. Also, when too much money is circulating in the economy due to oversupply, purchasing power falls, further creating inflation.

As far as the stock market and inflation go, their relationship is anything but straightforward and without a one-size-fits-all rule. However, some practices help mitigate the risks of inflation. For instance, stock investors typically use shares to hedge their portfolios from inflation over time. How this works is that a portfolio's or stock's value may appreciate during periods of inflation such that its purchasing power remains unaffected regardless of increasing prices.

> As far as the stock market and inflation go, their relationship is anything but straightforward and without a one-size-fits-all rule.

For example, when high input costs trigger inflation, the moment companies get their ducks in a row, make price adjustments, and adapt to the pressures of an inflationary economy, normal profit returns could resume even as revenues increase.

Deflation

Unlike inflation, deflation isn't a frequently occurring event. It

is indicated by an influx of products and services into the market and typically occurs when lower demand triggers substantial price drops. Deflation best describes times of economic depression and widespread unemployment, such as the Great Depression and other similar events.

Deflation indicates an economy with frequently falling prices of consumer goods. Although deflation sounds like a dreamy event, with falling prices and potentially higher availability of products and services, consumers are often hesitant to make purchases. And the longer the delay continues, the higher the supply of goods and services will be because less spending brings lower income, and producers may try to navigate the situation and remain profitable by cutting costs. That means higher unemployment rates as workers are let go. But this only creates a negative feedback loop that plummets prices further, making consumers even less likely to spend and compounding deflation with severe economic repercussions.

Although asset prices plummet in deflationary economies, certain types of investment have proved immune historically, performing better than others. For instance, stocks from top consumer staples sectors, like Walmart (WMT), continued to reflect positive returns in 2008, regardless of the deflationary environment. Consumer staples refer to non-discretionary items such as medical supplies, household products, and food—which are crucial to the survival of consumers and, thus, not reasonably delayed like other products and services.

Similarly, some bonds may also do well during deflation, often because the value of existing bond coupons increases. In some regions, many investors put all their funds into minerals like gold. They consider it a safe asset class for riding out market risks and uncertainties until deflationary markers subside.

Other factors that may influence the stock market are pretty numerous, such as political influences, the earnings of the corporation, natural disasters, or those caused by humans, amongst others. It is not advisable—I would not recommend that anyone, especially individual investors who are just beginning their journey in the finance world, rely so much on economic factors. I would only advise that you approach investment having at the back of your mind the possible convergence of different economic indicators; so you can have an objective view of the direction the stock market is about to take. It is safe to say that despite not being able to predict the next turn a stock market takes accurately, it is better to have at least an idea of how to weather the storm.

Key Takeaways

- As the prices of financial securities plummet during inflation, cash intrinsically increases in value.

- Rising inflation rates are costly and affect the economy, consumers, and financial markets.

- Elevated inflation leads to increased stock volatility.

- Consumers are less likely to withhold spending on necessary staples like food, healthcare, and household products in deflationary situations.

- It only becomes a trade war when other countries return the favor to the country that first initiates import tariffs or quotas.

- GDP shows whether or not a country's economy is performing well. A rising GDP is positive and welcomed, while a falling GDP spells economic disaster.

Economic factors can be vital knowledge when investing in stocks. As long as you have a good understanding of how the factors can influence the market, it becomes easier to take actionable steps and make sure you are not on the wrong end of the situation. The next chapter explores the kinds of investment strategies there are and the practical steps that will aid a good decision-making process when duly implemented.

Chapter 5

Investment Strategies

All intelligent investing is value investing.

–Charlie Munger

Investments are only a lucrative and smart measure to secure and maximize wealth when particular strategies are duly implemented. You can only get real value for whatever security you are investing in when you know exactly what you are doing and can make intelligent moves based on that knowledge.

In this chapter, we will explore how to invest in the stock market, including how to pick great stocks, the best time for investing, helpful tips, market terminology you should know, and why, among other things.

Picking the Right Stocks

There isn't a one-size-fits-all strategy for picking stocks that guarantees all profits and no risks. Many factors go into the ultimate strategy, including the desired outcome, risk tolerance, available capital, timing, and investment duration, among other things.

There is another core factor that just about surpasses the elements mentioned above: the purpose of a portfolio. Every investor enters the market with a different portfolio and different targets. While the common goal of investing is to make money, investors focus on it differently. For instance, some might want to make money to preserve their wealth, while others might want it for capital appreciation, retirement, and yet another for income supplementation.

Whatever the case, these elements drive investors and their stock choices. However, regardless of their differences, a few things are valid for the more successful investors and how they pick stocks:

- **Do your homework**: Understand that investing is business. So, you must commit to the technical and fundamental analysis of a stock to assess its fair value and learn the prospects of the issuing organization to ensure that they are in line with your goals and overall strategy.

- **Risk spread**: Thoroughly diversifying your portfolio is key to hedging against risk and complementing the shortcomings of one stock with others.

- **Portfolio building**: Apply qualitative and quantitative shock analysis when choosing stocks for your portfolio.

- **Emotional investing**: The financial securities market isn't open to sentimental decision-making. Do not be tempted to buy a stock because of market hype, and certainly don't rush into buying or selling based on market chatter.

The Best Time of the Day to Buy Stocks

Once the market opens in the morning, it's customary for prices and market volumes to go haywire. Opening hours apply to every market factor triggered by needed releases and events after the previous day's close. This pushes the market into peak volatility. Experienced traders might be able to sniff out favorable patterns within the mess to make some quick profits, particularly day traders, whose prime time begins within the first 15 minutes of the market's opening. However, the less-trained eye would be more susceptible to the whims of the market and wind up incurring significant losses. So, as a newbie trader, it's best to avoid opening hours, at least for a good hour.

Between 9:30 a.m. and 10:30 a.m. EST is perfect for day trading, and offering significant moves in little time. As the time runs down, however, and tapers towards 11:30 a.m., day traders start to close shop as volume plummets and volatility kicks in again. Now, moves are smaller, volume is lower, and trades take forever.

For people in the market for actively traded index ETFs and index futures, like the S&P 500 SPDR and the S&P 500 E-Minis, respectively, trading is on from the premarket (8:40 a.m.) and starts to taper off as the clock winds down on 10:30 a.m. Investors can continue to trade well until 11:30 a.m., so long as there are still opportunities in the market to leverage.

Four Tips to Help Navigate the Best Time to Buy Stocks

1. **Create and follow up on your goals**: Don't go into the market without a game plan. Have targets for your portfolio and be determined to make them work. Your goals could be to make a profit or learn more about a specific market sector.

2. **Consult a tax professional**: If you actively trade with a taxable brokerage account, you must pay capital gains tax, which will take a massive chunk of your gross returns. Having a professional on hand can help navigate mistakes that would otherwise be costly.

3. **Learn about your limitations**: Successful traders pray to be right more often than they are wrong. You must plan for when losses happen, so you don't get disillusioned and ruin other financial plans.

4. **Diversification is critical**: You want to maintain some balance in your portfolio so that it doesn't descend into chaos during active trading. Diversification is the key to managing losses and making a profit even when several market sectors hit a downtrend.

Methods to Raise Capital as an Investor

There are several methods that investors can use to raise capital for investing. Some of the most common ways include:

- **Personal savings**: Investors can use their savings to fund their investment activities. This can include money saved in a bank account, money invested in a retirement account, or other financial assets. Of course, dipping your hands into your savings can be challenging, especially since you assume all the risk yourself and could potentially lose your investments.

- **Borrowing**: Investors can also borrow money to fund their investment activities. This can include taking out a loan from a bank, borrowing from friends or family, or using a margin account with a broker. Borrowing means sharing risks with others who trust you with their funds; it also allows you access to more money than you could raise on your own.

- **Crowdfunding**: This is raising money by asking many people to contribute to a pool for a specific cause, usually through the internet. Crowdfunding has recently become popular and is a very effective way to raise capital, assuming you can convince the general public to donate generously.

- **Credit**: The investor can finance their investments on credit, usually provided by credit companies. This is generally in the form of credit cards, which can be used to pay for investments.

- **Selling assets**: Investors can sell assets, such as stocks or real estate, to generate capital for investing.

- **Investment products**: Investors can also use investment products, such as mutual funds or ETFs, to raise capital. These products allow investors to pool their money together and invest in a diversified portfolio of securities.

- **Fundraisers**: Investors can engage interested parties and convince them to donate to the cause. While this may seem similar to crowdfunding, the significant difference is that the donations are made by individuals who have a connection to the investor rather than the general public, as is found in crowdfunding.

- **Initial public offering (IPO)**: Companies can also raise capital by going public through an IPO. IPOs refer to the first time that businesses allow the public to purchase their shares.

- **Debt financing**: Companies can also raise capital by issuing debt securities, such as bonds, to investors. This allows the company to borrow money from investors in exchange for the promise of future interest payments and principal repayment.

Gilts

Government bonds issued by the UK government sometimes referred to as "gilt-edged securities," are traded on the gilts market (Merrill Edge, n.d.). Because they are backed by the full confidence and credit of the government, these bonds, which are issued to raise money for the government, are regarded as reasonably secure investments. Gilts are frequently issued with fixed coupon rates, which guarantee the investor a certain amount of interest until the bond expires. The UK government relies heavily on the gilt market as a source of finance, and the market is essential to the country's financial system. For investors searching for a comparatively secure and reliable investment, it is also a significant market.

There are a few key things you should consider if you are thinking about investing in the gilt market:

- **Risk**: Gilts are considered to be a relatively low-risk investment because they are backed by the full faith and credit of the UK government. However, it is still important to consider the overall risk profile of your investment portfolio and how gilts fit into it.

- **Yield**: The yield on gilts is the return you can expect to receive on your investment. The yield will depend on the current market conditions and the terms of the particular gilt you are considering. It is important to compare the yields on different gilts and consider whether they are sufficient for your investment goals.

- **Maturity**: Gilts have different maturities, which is the length of time until the bond must be repaid. It is important to consider the maturity of gilt and how it fits into your investment horizon. For example, if you are planning to use the money from your investment in the near future, you may want to consider shorter-term gilts.

- **Taxes**: The interest you receive on gilts is subject to UK income tax. It is important to consider the tax implications of investing in gilts and how they may affect your overall return on investment.

Overseas Shares

Overseas shares refer to stocks that are traded on a foreign stock exchange rather than a domestic (local) exchange. For example, if you are based in the United States, and you purchase shares in a company that is listed on the London Stock Exchange, you would be investing in overseas shares.

Investing in overseas shares can be a way to diversify your investment portfolio and potentially earn higher returns. It can also give you exposure to different economies and industries around the world. However, investing in overseas shares can also come with additional risks, such as currency exchange rate fluctuations and potential political and economic instability in the country where the company is based.

To invest in overseas shares, you may need to open a brokerage account that allows you to trade on foreign exchanges. You may also need to consider the tax implications and fees associated with investing in overseas shares. It is important to carefully research and evaluate the risks and potential rewards of investing in overseas shares before making any investment decisions.

There are a few things you should consider before investing in overseas shares:

- **Research the company and the market**: As with any investment, it is important to thoroughly research the company you are considering investing in. Look at the company's financial statements, management team, and industry trends to get a sense of its financial health and potential for growth. It is also important to understand the economic and political environment in the country where the company is based, as these factors can impact the performance of the company's stock.

- **Understand the risks**: Investing in overseas shares can come with additional risks, such as currency exchange rate fluctuations and potential political and economic instability in the country where the company is based. It is important to be aware of these risks and consider how they may affect the performance of your investment.

- **Consider the fees and taxes**: Investing in overseas shares may come with additional fees, such as brokerage fees and currency exchange fees. It is important to understand the fees associated with your investment and consider how they may impact your returns. You should also be aware of the tax implications of investing in overseas shares.

There are both risks and advantages associated with investing in overseas shares; it is important to carefully consider the risks and advantages of investing in overseas shares before making any investment decisions. It will be helpful to do your due diligence by doing proper research to understand the potential risks and rewards of investing in overseas shares and to make informed investment decisions.

Short Selling

Short selling is a trading strategy that involves selling securities that the trader does not own with the expectation that the price will fall. The trader borrows the securities from someone else and sells them on the market, hoping to buy them back later at a lower price. If the price does indeed fall, the trader can buy the securities back at the lower price, return them to the lender, and pocket the difference as profit.

Let's say, for example, that Alice predicts a decline in the value of a particular stock. She borrows 200 shares of the stock from Bob and sells them for $4,000 by selling them for $20 each on the open market. If the stock price really does drop to $10 per share, Alice can purchase the 200 shares again for $2,000, give them back to Bob, and keep the $2,000 profit.

However, Alice might end up with a loss if the stock price increases instead of declining. For instance, if the share price rises to $60, Alice would have to spend $12,000 to purchase the 200 shares back before she could give them to Bob. In this case, Alice would have to pay $8,000 out of her own pocket to close out the short position, resulting in a loss. Short selling can be a risky strategy, and it is not suitable for all investors. It is important to carefully consider the potential risks and rewards before attempting to short any securities.

There are several factors that an investor should consider before shorting security:

- **Risk tolerance**: Short selling involves the potential for significant losses, so it is important to have a high-risk tolerance and be prepared for the possibility of substantial losses.

- **Market conditions**: It is important to carefully evaluate the market conditions and consider whether the security you are considering short selling is likely to decrease in value.

- **Borrowing costs**: When short selling a security, you will typically have to borrow the security from someone else, and this may come with borrowing costs. It is important to consider these costs and whether they will eat into your potential profits.

- **Short interest**: The level of short interest in security (i.e., the number of shares that have been sold short as a percentage of the total number of shares outstanding) can have an impact on the price of the security. A high level of short interest may indicate that there is a lot of bearish sentiment about the security, which could potentially drive the price down further.

- **Dividends**: If the security you are short selling pays dividends, you will be required to pay the dividend to the lender of the security. This is an additional cost that you should consider when deciding whether to short security.

- **Regulations**: Some countries have regulations that limit or restrict the ability to short certain securities. It is important to familiarize yourself with these regulations and ensure that you are in compliance with them when short selling.

- **Margin requirements**: Short selling often requires the use of margin, which means that you will have to have enough money in your account to cover any potential losses. It is important to consider the margin requirements and whether you have sufficient funds to meet them.

Options Trading

Options trading is a financial activity that involves buying and selling options contracts. Options are traded on a variety of financial platforms, including stock exchanges and over-the-counter marketplaces. They are used to bet on market direction, hedge against future price swings, and create revenue. Two kinds of options exist, and they're named "call" and "put."

A call option grants the holder the right to purchase the underlying asset at a predetermined price, whereas a put option grants the holder the right to sell the underlying asset at a predetermined price. The strike price is the price at which the underlying asset can be bought or sold (Gordon, 2021).

Options traders can benefit from options trading by employing a variety of tactics. Buying and holding options, selling options (also known as "writing options"), and spreading or combining options are all frequent tactics (such as buying and selling options at different strike prices or with different expiration dates). Options trading can be complicated and dangerous. Before engaging in options trading, traders should have a full understanding of the underlying asset and market circumstances, as well as the mechanics of options and the related risks and potential rewards.

Here are some key things you should know before you start trading options:

- **Options basics**: You should have a basic understanding of how options work, including the difference between call options and put options, the terms "strike price" and "expiration date," and the concept of buying and selling options.

- **Risk management**: Options trading involves significant risk, including the risk of losing the entire amount invested. It is important to understand and manage this risk by setting appropriate position sizes and using stop-loss orders.

- **Market conditions**: Options prices are affected by various market factors, including the underlying asset's price, market volatility, and the time remaining until the option expires. It is important to understand these factors and how they can affect the value of your options positions.

- **Trading strategies**: There are many different options

trading strategies that you can use, each with its own risk and reward profile. It is important to understand the potential outcomes and risks of each strategy before using it in your trading.

- **Brokerage platform**: You will need to choose a brokerage platform that offers options trading and provides the tools and resources you need to research and trade options.

- **Trading psychology**: Trading options can be emotionally challenging, as it involves making decisions under uncertainty and managing risk. It is important to have a clear understanding of your own risk tolerance and to trade in a disciplined and logical manner.

Options trading is not suitable for all investors, and it is important to carefully consider your investment objectives, risk tolerance, and financial situation before engaging in this activity. It is also important to work with a reputable broker and to use sound risk management practices to help mitigate the risks of options trading.

Penny Stocks

These stocks are often associated with small, young, or financially unstable companies, and they tend to be very volatile, meaning that their prices can fluctuate significantly over short periods of time. Because of their low prices and how speculative they can be, penny stocks are quite risky.

There are a few key characteristics that differentiate penny stocks from other types of stocks. OTC markets are less regulated and have lower trading volumes than major exchanges, which can make it more difficult to find buyers or sellers for penny stocks.

Second, penny stocks are often issued by small, relatively unknown companies that do not have a proven track record of success. These companies may be struggling to generate revenue or may not have a clear plan for how they will turn a profit. As a result, investing in penny stocks carries a higher level of risk than investing in more established companies.

Finally, penny stocks are known for their high volatility, meaning that their prices can fluctuate dramatically over short periods of time. This can be caused by a number of factors, including changes in market conditions, changes in the company's financial health, or the influence of individual investors or groups of investors.

While it is possible to make a profit from penny stocks, they are generally considered to be high-risk investments and are not suitable for everyone. If you are considering investing in penny stocks, it is essential to do your research and carefully evaluate the risks and potential rewards before making a decision.

There are a few key things that you should consider before investing in penny stocks:

- **Understand the risks**: The companies that issue penny stocks are often small and financially unstable, and their stocks can be highly volatile. It is important to understand the risks associated with penny stocks and to be prepared for the possibility of losing all or part of your investment.

- **Do your research**: It is important to thoroughly research the company and its financial health before investing in a penny stock. Look for information about the company's management team, its business model, and its financial performance. Consider seeking the advice of a financial professional or consulting with a financial advisor before making a decision.

- **Be aware of potential scams**: Penny stocks are often the target of fraud and manipulation. Be on the lookout for signs of a potential scam, such as unrealistic promises of high returns or pressure to buy quickly.

- **Be prepared for volatility**: Penny stocks are known for their high volatility, which means that their prices can fluctuate significantly over short periods of time. Be prepared for the possibility of significant price swings and have a plan in place for how you will handle these fluctuations.

If you are considering investing in penny stocks, it is essential to do your research and carefully evaluate the risks and potential rewards before making a decision.

Value Investing

Value investing involves purchasing stocks trading at a

significantly lower price than they are intrinsically worth. To do this, investors study the market and identify companies with low valuation metrics, often low multiples of their assets or profits, for reasons that become inexplicable over time. To be a value investor, you ought to have differing opinions from the market and the patience to watch your investments blossom in the long run.

In the last century, value investing has consistently outperformed index returns across many stock markets. Value stocks aren't sold at a discount because the market isn't wiser. Many factors come into play that may trigger significant drops in share prices, with profit disappointments in the short term being the most common answer. Often, these disappointments result in strong emotional reactions in which shareholders dump the stock for fear that more negative developments might follow.

Value investing is founded on the premise of ownership. If you purchase a company's stock, you are now a part owner of the business. Of course. That goes without saying. Yet, it's not uncommon for investors to secure stock in a bid to play the market, not minding the underlying fundamentals of their companies.

To determine a company's intrinsic value, you first have to figure out the current value of its future cash flow. That, in turn, can be determined by evaluating future cash flows and the interest rate used to assess the current cash flows' values. Using these metrics, it makes sense why intrinsic values are expressed in a range instead of precise figures.

Growth Investing

Unlike value stocks, growth stocks are already in promising positions, and they are found in emerging industry niches. Due to the appealing potentials they hold, coupled with the uncommon success the company has enjoyed recently, growth stocks go for premiums. This price point also indicates investors' optimism in the company. As such, it's easy to point outgrowth stocks. Identify stocks whose valuations, particularly their price-to-earnings multiples, are higher than their industry counterparts and the market at large.

This appears to be the inherent risk with growth stocks: purchasing and holding them isn't cheap. Nonetheless, investors who prefer this stock don't look at the current cost. Instead, their eyes are on future growth, which promises returns for years to come. To them, that's a worthwhile justification for the premium price point.

Another risk with growth stocks is that since the issuing companies reinvest their earnings in further growth and expansion, dividends are out of the question—but only until growth starts to plateau or slow down.

With these implications, growth investing isn't suited to investors who are averse to risk or in the market for quick returns. Instead, they are best used by people with long-term mindsets, longer investment timelines, and higher risk tolerances.

Dollar Cost Averaging

Dollar-cost averaging is investing the same amount into a particular stock at regular intervals for a given time frame, regardless of price fluctuations. This strategy allows investors to decrease their average cost for each share they own, thereby hedging their portfolios against volatility.

Essentially, the strategy removes the need to time the market to identify opportunities for good trades frequently. For example, if you invest $150 every month into the same index fund over four months, the number of shares you get each time will differ based on price changes. Say that for the first month, the cost per share was $3, then it increased to $5 in the second month, fell to $2 in the third month, and rose to $3.5 in the fourth month. By the end of this four-month timeline, your total investment will be $600. You would have a total of 197 shares. Since the average price of shares for all four months is $3.38, your ROI would be $690. That is a $90 profit across four months.

It's crucial to determine the average price per share and compare it against the average cost per share you wind up paying. For this example, the average share price across all four months was:

3 + 5 + 2 + 3.5 = $3.38.

Albeit, you paid cheaper for the average cost of each share:

$600 ÷ 197 = $3.04

Of course, it's not a given that using this strategy is a sure bet for profits, nor is it the perfect protection against share price drops.

Who Needs Dollar Cost Averaging?

- Dollar-cost averaging is best suited for investors interested in leveraging its perks: automatic frequent investing over given time intervals, potentially lower average costs, and the freedom from deciding under duress when the market is highly volatile.

- This strategy might also be handy for new investors who are still learning the ropes and want to improve their judgment of the best moments to make purchases.

- Long-term investors may also find dollar-cost averaging a reliable technique, especially if they want to invest frequently but can't study the market and time price shifts.

Bear Market vs. Bull Market

Bull markets are periods when stocks appreciate (typically a 20% or more increase over two months), and the overall sentiment of the market is favorable. The increase in stock value during a bull market indicates strong economic standing, expansion, and feelings of confidence and optimism among investors.

Conversely, "bear markets" are periods of plummeting stock prices, with market sentiment seemingly negative. Drops indicate bear markets in the broad market index by 20% or more across two months.

The Differences

- **Gross Domestic Product (GDP) Changes**: Bear markets often indicate that the economy is slowing down, which could make the populace less likely to spend. All of these culminate in reduced GDP. However, during bull markets, companies experience higher revenue generation, which causes the economy to grow as consumers are more willing to spend.

- **Unemployment**: During a bull market, when companies grow and take in higher revenues, they may need a longer workforce and have the funds to invest. This would contribute to managing unemployment in the population. However, in bear markets, companies are more likely to reduce their workforce to cut costs and avoid hiring more hands.

- **Demand and supply**: More people are willing to buy securities during bull markets because they have purchased power and the economy is in good standing. This leads to securities appreciating. However, when the market turns bearish, investors try to sell off their assets to recoup some capital and cut their losses quickly.

Key Takeaways

- Dollar-cost averaging will help you get good deals on securities over time, but it doesn't guarantee profitability every time.

- Bull markets represent good tidings for the economy and the population, while bear markets are terrible.

- Value investing is buying securities sold at a fraction of their actual values. Investors like these stocks because they believe that the tide could turn.

- Everyone already believes in growth stocks. They have such a high price point, and issuing companies are committed to maintaining that status.

- The best time for trading is between 8:30 a.m. and 11:30 a.m. EST, depending on the type of trader you are.

- Choosing the right stock largely depends on your plans for your portfolio and your investing goals.

    Choosing the right stock largely depends on your plans for your portfolio and your investing goals.

The next chapter will analyze value investing and what makes a stock valuable.

Chapter 6

Value Investing

Value Investing is the discipline of buying securities at a significant discount from their current underlying values and holding them until more of their value is realized. The element of a bargain is the key to the process.

—Seth Klarman

This chapter will help you understand what value investing is, the right strategies needed to utilize it, and the risks that are attached to this method.

A long-term investor might, before investing in a company, look for its growth potential. In this case, an investor like this can be said to practice growth investing. On the other hand, if the investor seeks out companies whose prices are below their fair value, it is called value investing.

What Is Value Investing?

The idea behind value investing is to cash in on the potential appreciation of a company's shares.

Understand the Power of Compounding

The more time you allow for your investment to mature, the greater the likelihood it will increase in value and earn you a sizable profit.

Understanding the Margin of Safety

The margin of safety is the value that's gotten when the market price of an investment is subtracted from its value. It represents the cushion that an investor has to protect against potential declines in the value of an investment.

For example, if an investor believes that a stock is worth $100 per share based on its underlying fundamentals, but it is currently trading at $80 per share, the investor has a margin of safety of $20 per share. This means that if the stock's value falls, the investor has a buffer of $20 per share to protect against losses.

Investors who use a margin of safety approach aim to buy assets at a significant discount to their intrinsic value in order to reduce the risk of losing money. The goal is to give the investment time to appreciate in value and eventually reach its intrinsic value, at which point the investor can sell the investment for a profit.

The margin of safety is a strategy that sees investors acquiring undervalued assets. By looking for investments with a large margin of safety, value investors aim to minimize risk and maximize returns.

What Makes a Great Stock?

Profits

It should go without saying that a company's stock is only valuable to an investor if it has the potential to yield substantial returns. This is the first and most important rule when choosing a stock: Will it make you more money than you've invested?

Low Debt Ratio

A profitable stock should have a low debt-to-income ratio. Although a company receives its financing from loans, it must be able to repay its debts comfortably. Companies with higher obligations have lower stock values because, when things go wrong, they may find it challenging to repay their debts and, consequently, their investors.

Quality Products

Research has it that companies with innovative products have great stock values. So, if you're an investor, I would advise you to look in that direction. An obsessive client base enriches these companies. They do not need to take on more debt to expand or do well in business. An example is Netflix.

Good Management

A company with good management has great stock value. Companies with lousy management often flop at the end of the day. An example is Bellamy's (BAL), whose shares dropped from $11.88 to $6.71 in a day.

Intrinsic Value and Value Investment

Intrinsic value has been mentioned in this text, and you might be curious about what it is. Intrinsic value is the measurement of the worth of an asset. Although comparing the current market price of an asset to the intrinsic value of the same asset gives investors insight as to whether it's overvalued or undervalued, it is not the same as intrinsic value.

Knowing the intrinsic value of an investment helps people understand the right time to invest in a stock.

Determining Intrinsic Value With the Price-to-Book Ratio

The price-to-book ratio serves as a measure of the market value of a company based on its book value. Book value, on the other hand, is the carrying value of an asset on a balance sheet. A company's book value is often calculated by netting its assets against its accumulated depreciation.

To calculate the book value per share, you have to know the total assets of the company, its total liabilities, and the number of outstanding shares. When these values are known, you can determine a company's book value using the formula below:

(total assets − total liabilities) ÷ number of outstanding shares = book value per share

On the other hand, the market value per share is obtained by checking the share price quote in the market.

So, to determine the price-to-book ratio of a company, you have to divide the book value per share by its market value per share.

BV/S ÷ MV/S = P/BR

Markets Are Not Efficient

In value investing, one has to note that sometimes markets are not efficient. Market efficiency refers to how well or not market prices reveal all accessible and applicable information about the value of assets. In a situation where the quality of data rises, the market becomes efficient, thereby decreasing the chances of arbitrage and above-market returns.

However, in the real sense of the word, markets cannot be relied on due to their inefficiency. An inefficient market does not accurately reflect the actual value of assets. This results from many factors, such as information asymmetries, cost of transactions, human emotions, etc.

Do Not Follow the Herd

The instinct of humans to be part of the crowd in conformity with the behaviors and beliefs of a larger percentage of people poses a challenge to one's ability to make good and correct decisions. We often trust and rely on the wisdom of large groups in choosing the right phone, restaurant, etc. It is the same in investing, depending on most people's opinions.

When Warren Buffett said, "Be greedy when others are fearful and fearful when others are greedy," he spoke about the dangers of following the herd.

This stresses the importance of having the right team to discuss investment ideas.

Value Investing Requires Diligence

Estimating the intrinsic value of an asset sometimes involves an element of subjectivity on the part of the investor. Investors who look forward to earning from an asset bought below its intrinsic value have the duty to secure those assets until they reach their intrinsic value or, even better, soar above it.

These processes do not happen overnight, hence hinting at the importance for investors to put in their quota by being diligent.

Why Do Stocks Become Undervalued?

"Undervalued stocks" are shares or assets that are below their intrinsic value. This can occur due to a myriad of reasons.

When the Overall Market Is Down

The market suffers when the macroeconomic condition of the country is poor. Investors should, however, have a good knowledge of the country's economic state to determine the value of shares.

Overinvestment

This is why a good investor should avoid the herd mentality. When so many people are investing in a stock, the value of these stocks will fall, and the chances of it rising again are difficult.

Diversification

Businesses with new markets and disruptive products typically have undervalued stocks. In contrast, old companies that stick to their traditional business will likely remain at the same market price over time. Investors pick this up and buy shares from these new businesses.

Avoid Value Traps

In a bid to acquire underpriced assets, you should know that cheap stocks may not always mean sound investments. Do not fall for value traps!

Long-term investment pays off so long as you can buy quality stocks at reasonable prices and wait patiently. How do you determine what asset has good value? You have to do your homework well. For instance, check what catalyst might cause

the stock's rise in the future.

Value Investing Strategies

- **Put your money into businesses you can comprehend**: You should be able to make well-informed guesses about the company you are investing in. So, if you don't know what a company does, you have no business buying shares from them.

- **Invest in well-managed companies**: A well-managed company adds value to a company, while lousy management, irrespective of their assets, can destroy a company.

- **Do not stress over-diversification**: Stick to the few stocks you've thoroughly researched and invested in, and be at peace with them, then stress over putting your funds in so many stocks.

- **Your best investment should serve as a guide**: In any situation where you have more investment capital, you shouldn't aim for diversity. Instead, aim at opportunities that beat your previous investment.

Couch Potato Investment

As the name suggests, couch potato investing is a passive investment. A couch potato investor automates their

investments. This sort of investment is for people who have a low-maintenance investment strategy. You get long-term gains by setting up minimal management.

The Risk of Value Investing

- **Falling into value traps**: We previously mentioned what value traps are. Since buying assets when they're cheap is often the preferred strategy of many investors, it is important to remember that not all that glitters is gold. It would be best if you made extensive inquiries regarding a stock before jumping on it.

- **Unforeseen circumstances**: Situations like lawsuits or natural disasters may negatively impact the gains an investor can make from a company.

- **Buying overvalued stocks**: Sometimes, value investors find themselves in a situation where they pay too much for a stock. You stand a chance of losing part or all of your money. The same goes for investors who buy stocks slightly below their market price.

Benjamin Graham Case Study

Benjamin Graham was born in London, UK, in 1894. His work is foundational in stock analysis. By the age of 25, he had made up to $500,000. However, he lost a lot of money during the stock market crash of 1925.

Benjamin Graham laid a foundation for value investors and firmly believed that the market is efficient or else the point of value investing would be useless.

He wrote many books, including The Intelligent Investor, which is every value investor's manual.

Warren Buffett Case Study

Warren Buffett is a big investing guru starting at the early age of eleven. He read several books on investments, and today he is one of the wealthiest people in the world, with a net worth of over $104 billion. He was a student of Benjamin Graham before he left and started his own investment company. His business prospered as he applied Graham's lessons, and he became a millionaire before the age of thirty.

After closing down his company, Graham went about a new strategy based on the principle of finding undervalued equity shares no one knew about.

Warren Buffett has said on so many occasions that he does not know what the economy will be like in the next month, year, or decade. Still, he is sensitive enough to note where the market valuation is in contrast to historical valuation.

Key Takeaways

- Value investing means buying stocks at an underpriced value.

- Profitability, low debt ratio, quality products, and good management determine a good stock value.

- Intrinsic value serves as a yardstick for measuring the worth of an asset.

- (Total assets − total liabilities) ÷ the number of outstanding shares = book value per share.

- Value investors don't follow the herd, avoid value traps, and are diligent.

- Couch Potato Investment means buying and securing assets for which someone has done the investment analysis.

In the next chapter, we are going to discover another form of investment that investors put into consideration before buying a stock.

Chapter 7

Growth Investing

It's not how right or wrong you are that matters but how much money you make when you're right and how much money you lose when you're wrong.

–George Soros

They say we've got our lives assigned to us by fate, especially regarding who becomes rich or stays poor. This is a passive approach to life and business that may not be based on facts. You can improve a lot in life, and one way to do so is by investing your money.

> They say we've got our lives assigned to us by fate, especially regarding who becomes rich or stays poor.

In this chapter, we will discuss growth investing, the different types of this strategy, how to evaluate a company's potential for growth, and terms like "strong historical earnings growth," "strong forward earnings growth," "strong profit margins," "strong return on equity," and "strong stock performance." You'll also learn the difference between growth investing and value investing, which was discussed in the last chapter.

What Is Growth Investing?

Growth investment is another investment aiming to increase an investor's capital. Growth investors buy "growth stocks" from companies. These growth stocks are related to new companies whose income is expected to increase. Growth investing favors small businesses, especially ones that have excellent prospects of becoming better and generating above-average profits in the future, for instance, companies in fast-growing industries like technology.

Understanding Growth Investing

When a company opens, it has a lot of potential, and for that potential to be actualized, it may need funds. This is where investors come in. Investors look for young businesses with impressive prospects, especially in thriving sectors where new technologies are being introduced and old ones improved.

Growth investors gain when these companies have expanded and prospered in the future, and the stocks they invested must have increased with higher prices in the market. They often reinvest their profits to make newer technologies to put them ahead of their competitors.

Growth investing is often juxtaposed with value investing, where value investors buy undervalued stocks while growth investors buy stocks from companies they think have the potential for capital appreciation. Investors have to put in a lot of work in looking for and studying the patterns of companies to decipher how well they would do in the future and have the potential to compete with other and even bigger companies favorably.

There is a high risk in growth investment because these companies are relatively new and have not been tried out before, and the chances of them flopping are there. But on the other hand, there are chances they will outgrow their competitors and produce higher returns shortly.

Popular Types of Growth Investment

The sectors listed below have proven over time to possess a high chance of yielding profits, which accounts for their popularity.

Small Cap Stocks

Small cap companies, also known as "small capitalization" companies, have a stock value of about $300 million to $2 billion, although they vary. They are called small cap because the totality of their estimated worth in the market at the time is relatively small compared to more prominent industries.

These are young companies with the potential to do better in the future. This is because they are still at their initial stage of growth. Thereby, their stocks have the potential for appreciation in the future. For this reason, they are one of the most popular stocks.

Technology and Healthcare Stocks

Healthcare and the technological sector go hand in hand since the healthcare sector develops new technologies to solve health problems. An example is the development of MRI machines to detect cancer or other unusual growths in the body. There are also other technological advancements to solve medical issues.

Companies concerned with technology frequently introduce new and improved software and hardware. The customer base for such companies is always eager to try new technology. As such, investors are advised to buy stocks from sectors like this.

Speculative Investments

Investing in high-risk investments such as futures and cryptocurrencies does not have a guaranteed return. This means that the value of assets in such sectors may be favorable one day and then suddenly take a turn for the worse.

What to Look for in Growth Investing

Growth investing requires individual judgment, as when adherents of this strategy apply whatever criteria they have, they also have to focus on the company's situation—comparing the company in question with its industry's past performance. Therefore, the guideline varies between companies and industries. These factors should be at the back of every growth investor's mind:

- **Increase in quarterly sales**: This gives investors an idea of the company's quarterly sales growth. They compare the increase in sales made by a company after a quarter of the year to the same quarter the year before.

- **Consistent sales growth ratio annually**: Growth investors use this factor to select stocks whose sales growth increases yearly. A company is considered healthy if it keeps introducing new products to the market, diversifies its business while changing its technologies, and meets the needs of its customers (e-earners).

- **Quarterly EBITDA growth**: EBITDA in full means Earnings Before Interest, Taxes, Depreciation, and Amortization. This measures the profits a business gets before any form of indebtedness follows mandatory payments and costs required to maintain its asset base. That way, growth investors know how much cash a company makes from its business.

- **Quarterly net profit growth**: This shows that a company can generate profit after deducting its revenue.

- **Consistent increase in quarterly earnings per share (EPS)**: This indicates a company's EPS. How much are the company's earnings per share every quarter of the year? Compare the earnings of one quarter to another to check the increase.

- **The consistent increase of annual EPS**: When you compare this year's earnings per share to those of last year, is there a significant increase?

- **Increasing cash flow from operations**: If, after deducting costs spent on the distribution and production of goods, there is still enough cash to maintain their operations, you should watch that company.

Evaluating a Company's Potential for Growth

Revenue and Earnings

Revenue means the total money made by a company after carrying out business operations, while earnings are periodic profits made by a business. The most common feature or sign of growth in a company is its revenue growth. A company with a high EPS is considered profitable, and investors are encouraged to buy shares from these companies.

Price-to-Earnings Ratios

This is a widely used scale for measuring a company's performance, indicating the market's estimation of the company's future growth prospects.

Return on Equity

It is one of the adequate metrics to assess a company's ability to benefit from its existing financial resources. It views earnings in contrast to shareholders' equity, which represents the money that would be achieved after the shares of shareholders are liquidated and returned to them.

Strong Historical Earnings Growth

"Historical earnings growth" measures how a stock's EPS has grown after five years. It tells growth investors how quickly a company's profits increase. A company expands its EPS by implementing the following measures: improving sales, reducing costs, or curtailing the number of shares outstanding in the marketplace. A company with strong historical earnings growth looks appealing to growth investors.

Strong Forward Earnings Growth

"Forward earnings" are an assessment of the successive term's earnings of a company, which is usually till the end of a fiscal year, sometimes to the beginning of the following year. This is important to growth investors because stock prices are supposed to reflect the prospects of future earnings discounted to the present. If there are strong prospects for an increase in earnings of a company, chances are investors should buy stocks from said company.

Strong Profit Margins

"Profit margins" are the amounts that remain after a company deducts its startup expenses from its earnings. It measures how profitable a company's pricing strategy is, how well they regulate its costs, and how efficiently they use raw materials and labor to manufacture its products or services. Profit margins, just like return on equity and the price-to-earnings ratio, measure the profitability of a company.

Strong Return on Equity

"Return on equity" has been discussed earlier. It was mentioned earlier that to check a company's profitability; investors have to focus on the company, other companies, and their industries. A strong return on equity determines if investors will buy stocks in a company. A strong stock is said to be 15%–20%.

A Step-By-Step Guide to Getting Started

These four steps will guide you on your journey as a growth investor:

Step 01: Prepare Your Finances

The first rule is not to invest cash you would need in the next five years. This is because, as much as the market rises over a long period, there could be sharp drops in stock prices of about

10%–20% with no warning. No one wants to go through the hurdle of selling their stocks during those downtimes. So, the advice is to buy stock with the cash you won't need for the next five years and more.

Step 02: Get comfortable With Growth Approaches

There are different growth investment approaches from which you can choose. You should learn about each one and stick with the most promising approach. For example, consider focusing on large and well-established companies with a history of generating profits.

As was stated in the previous chapter, you must invest in companies you are well aware of. Knowing these companies or industries would guide you in evaluating investments as potential buy customers.

The strength of a company is more important than the price of the stocks you get from it. Warren Buffett says, "It is better to buy a fair price from a wonderful company than from a fair company at a wonderful price."

Reading good investment books would go a long way in your investment journey—acquainting yourself with the investment gurus themselves.

Step 03: Stock Selection

This stage is about knowing the amount of cash you wish to allocate to your growth investment strategy. If you're new, it only makes sense to start small. The more you get comfortable with the whole process, building up your investing experience through different markets, you could increase your ratio.

Buying growth funds should be your main focus in your investment strategy since a lot of retirement plans focus on buying growth stocks. Index funds are another one. They deliver diversification at a lower cost compared to mutual funds. You could also buy individual growth stocks with prospects for market-beating returns. However, they are riskier than investing in a diversified fund.

Step 04: Maximize Returns

Growth investments can be unpredictable. While you should focus on holding your investment for several years, you also have to be keen on observing significant price changes.

- Where a portion of your holdings has gained a lot of value to the extent of dominating your portfolio, you might want to reduce your exposure. You could do that by rebalancing your portfolio.

- Where a stock rises above your estimated value, you could sell it and reinvest in a reasonably priced investment.

- If the company fails to meet your expectations or your investment thesis, you could sell its stock. A broken investment thesis could be a decline in pricing power and disruption by lower-priced competitors.

These are just a few of the many other reasons why an investor may want to sell their stock.

Growth Investing vs. Value Investing

Growth investors gain from the rapid price appreciation of growth stocks in the future rather than receiving dividends like large companies. Hence, they are widely volatile and unpredictable.

Value stocks, on the other hand, are steady throughout all market conditions as it takes time for them to gain in price. Value investors buy undervalued stocks and secure them for the foreseeable future. Since value stocks are stocks from companies on sale, a low price relative to profits makes them agree.

Notable investors like Warren Buffett think that there is no theoretical difference between the concepts of value investing.

Key takeaways

- Growth investors bet on "growth stocks," and they win when the price appreciates.

- Growth stock companies are usually found in the tech sector.

- Popular growth stocks include small cap, technology, healthcare, and speculative stocks.

- Growth investors focus on certain factors in evaluating companies, such as historical and projected earnings growth, return on equity, and profit margins.

In the next chapter, we'll discuss day trading and all you need to know to win by applying this strategy.

Chapter 8

Day Trading

The goal of a successful trader is to make the best trades. Money is secondary.

–Alexander Elder

In this chapter, we will carefully and factually analyze the basics of day trading, why it is controversial, how a day trader can get started, and a few strategies such as trend-following, mean reversion, scalping, and momentum trading. We'll also discuss, in great detail, the risks day traders face, what makes this venture difficult, and some solutions to help you succeed.

The Basics of Day Trading

Day trading has little connection with trading as it is conventionally known. It is defined as buying and selling securities within a day or seconds. It is simply manipulating the up-and-down price movement that occurs during a trading round. Investors who employ this strategy are often well-informed about even the minor details of trading and may have deep pockets. They are also familiar with events that cause short-term market moves, such as the news.

Successful day traders also deftly employ different strategies to make profits in the market. Some of these strategies include scalping, range trading, news trading, and high-frequency trading.

You may design your own trading platform; however, a good number of traders use a prepackaged platform setup provided by either their brokerage or a specialized software company.

A trader would typically utilize multiple screens to display charts and technical indicators that will provide buy and sell signals, hence the need to have a powerful desktop-based computer with at least two monitors.

While using a brokerage platform, you need to make sure real-time news and data feeds are included in the package. You will need such data to create charts that will reveal trends and depict the time frames and trading strategies you prefer.

Why Day Trading Is Controversial

"Day trading" is a controversial topic often discussed by financial experts. These issues have raised arguments about whether day trading is safe due to the risks and insecurity attached to it. Some of them include the following:

The potential of making a profit off day trading is often debated on Wall Street since it has, for lack of a better word, lured novices into the market with promises of making huge returns in a relatively short time. Sadly, such beginner traders aren't given much information on the risks involved in this business and how they can mitigate them.

Most investors do not have the money, time, or patience to go into something that could bring so much stress and loss. Financial advisors have argued that the gains at the end of the day in day trading do not justify the risks involved.

How Does a Day Trader Get Started?

During its popularity in the early 1900s, one did not necessarily require trading skills to succeed in this cutthroat venture. Selling internet stocks was relatively easy, and many people who identified as day traders at the time made massive returns. However, when it all declined between 1998 and 2000, a number of people pursued other businesses.

They discovered that, like other professions, day trading required some education and skill acquisition, for example:

- **Knowledge and experience of the marketplace**: Just like it was stated in the previous chapter on the need to know a company well before investing in its stocks, you cannot jump into day trading before learning all there is to know about it. Doing so may put you at risk of losing money since you do not have an understanding of the platform. Experience gives you an edge in day trading, and the more experience you have, the better you know what to avoid and what strategies to use while trading.

- **Sufficient capital**: Sufficient funds are needed for those who intend to employ leverage in margin accounts.

There are two types of day traders: professional day traders and individual day traders. Below are a few steps to get started as a day trader:

Open a Brokerage Account

Opening an account with a broker is important because a broker, whether a person or a company, conducts a myriad of research and trades; hence, they have correct information about what is trending in the marketplace and the performance of stocks in the market.

When you have an account with them, you will be provided with a great deal of information about the various stocks you might want to venture into, for instance, their price history, stock movements, technical information/indicators, etc.

Ensure Your Account Reaches the Equity Requirements

The Financial Industry Regulatory Authority, which encourages investors and traders to partake in the market, dictates the minimum equity requirement for a day trader. As such, day traders should have a margin account balance of no less than $25,000.

This is why day traders need to have sufficient capital before starting trading. This requirement is for the benefit of day traders, as having this money in your account would help cover any risk you come across.

Of course, this amount is not necessary to become an individual day trader, but it gives you an idea of the scale of funds required to make successful trades. That is, using $1,000 per trade and making a reasonable 2.8% gain only nets you $28—hardly enough to pay the brokerage cost. Even a 15% spike gain would only net you $150. Again, you would need dozens of these 15% spikes in a day just to make ends meet, and believe me; you'll be unlikely to find multiple 15% winning trades in a day!

Conduct a Minimum of Four Trades Within Five Days

Although some traders do not necessarily adhere to this rule, trading four times out of five days can be an effective practice for beginners new to the day trading space. Such frequency would help them gain experience that will be of immense value to them further on in their careers.

This is also one of the rules enacted by the Financial Industry Regulatory Authority (FINRA).

Become a Day Trading Team Member

If you do not want to invest too much of your own money, you should become a member of a day trading team. You'll be able to conduct transactions through such companies.

Day Trading Strategies

To be a day trader, you must be strategic and ready to work hard for it. One crucial skill needed to become a profitable trader is learning valuable techniques to accurately determine when to enter or exit the market. Many traders key into this and develop styles they stick to once they get comfortable with them. Some traders sell just one or two stocks per day, while others sell more of their favorite stocks per day. Some benefits of selling more stocks are that traders discover how to act under different conditions and how key market makers influence movements.

Below are other strategies a trader can employ toward successful trading.

Trending-Following Strategy

There are diverse techniques that can be employed to figure out market movements. Such an understanding would help investors create reliable trade signals. Day traders buy price trends when they go up and sell them when they go down.

> There are diverse techniques that can be employed to figure out market movements.

Day traders who use this strategy do not rely on forecasts to calculate the market price. They jump on whichever one happens to be trending.

Some of the best trend-following strategies include the moving average crossover trend trading strategy, the Boiler band strategy, the MACD crossover, and ascending and descending triangles.

Mean Reversion Strategy

The mean reversion strategy is an attempt to stake on extreme fluctuations in the pricing, volatility, growth, or technical indicators of a particular security or asset, assuming that it will regress to normal levels. Traders who exploit the mean reversion strategy have various methods for using it.

Scalping Strategy

This strategy helps investors make money from relatively tiny changes in price. With scalping, traders are expected to have stringent exit strategies. This is because one significant loss could render futile the many small gains that a trader has made. A successful scalping strategy always has a very high ratio of winning trades compared to losses.

Momentum Trading Strategy

Over the years, this strategy has proved to be quite effective in the financial market. It is more popular than the "buy low, sell high" strategy because it reveals securities that are not only on the rise but have also gained some momentum. This means that such assets are likely to continue their upward trend even after purchase.

Risks of Day Trading

- **Financial losses**: Day traders tend to be hit the hardest in their first few months of navigating the market, and sometimes they do not get the chance to soar to the heights of making a profit.

- **Day traders are not investors**: Given how volatile stocks are, day traders try to be on the safe side by selling stocks when their value increases and buying them when their value is rising or falling. This primarily occupies the time of a day trader, so they are not investors for fear of instant fluctuations, which could ruin them for a long time.

- **It is a stressful and expensive full-time job**: Day trading is highly stressful. As a result, traders have to be glued to their computer screens for a significant percentage of their time, monitoring the movement in the market. It requires maximum concentration and keeps traders on their toes most of the time. It is expensive because of the money traders pay their companies for commission, training, and the expenses for the computers they use.

- **There is some dependence on borrowing**: Someday, traders may find themselves in serious debt when they get loans to buy stocks but their investments fail. Such debts tend to snowball as they borrow even more funds to pay off their lenders.

- **Do not believe claims of easy profit**: Do not be deceived by advertisers who preach quick and sure ways to gain from day trading. Those hot tips and educational newsletters may not be objective or factual.

What Makes Day Trading Difficult?

- **Volatility**: Due to its volatile nature, day trading may be too demanding for most people.

- **Multiple catalysts**: A stock catalyst is something that influences the movement of a company's shares. Where this becomes a problem is when catalysts control financial securities. Multiple triggers are often difficult to decipher for a lot of people. Sometimes, stock prices decline after prior solid results.

- **Multiple concepts**: Day trading is a complicated venture because of the diverse range of concepts a person is required to learn. An example is the need to understand technical and fundamental analysis, both of which are complex subjects.

- **Impatience**: The get-rich-quick mentality hinders most traders from reaching their full potential, as they become impatient from the onset of their careers.

Day Trading Examples

Supposing investor A is a person who has an already established brokerage. Note that investor A uses the trend-following strategy and, as such, makes the following trades in a week:

- **Monday**: One-day trade
    - Bought 20 shares of BCD Healthcare Company and sold all 20 shares.
- **Tuesday**: One-day trade
    - Bought 55 shares of BOY, a group of companies, and sold all the shares.
- **Wednesday**: Two-day trade
    - Bought 100 shares of ADC Media and sold them all.
    - Bought 50 shares of JEK Computers and sold all of them.
- **Thursday**: Two-day trade
    - Bought 50 shares of BCD Healthcare and sold them all on the same day.
    - Bought 50 shares of ADC Media and sold them all.

Investor A has completed four trades within five days or less, representing more than 6% of their input trades. According to

FINRA, investor A is considered a day trader. For this reason, their brokerage will require them to maintain a $25,000 balance in their margin account.

Key Takeaways

- Day traders purchase securities and put them up for sale daily.

- Day trading is controversial because of the risks attached to it.

- Strategies used by day traders include the trend-following strategy, the mean-reversion strategy, the scalping strategy, and the momentum trading strategy.

- Day trading can be expensive and stressful, and traders often end up becoming debtors.

In the next chapter, we'll discuss a closely related and equally important topic: swing trading.

Chapter 9

Swing Trading

The trend is your best friend until it bends.

–Ed Seykota

One beautiful thing about life is choosing whatever works for us. You don't like to use the elevator? Fine, use the stairs. You don't want your coffee iced? Warm coffee might be a better option for you. We make choices daily and follow through with them; whether good or bad, we must be ready to accept the consequences. This analogy can be connected to trading. Certain individuals prefer the multiple opportunities made available by day trading, so they have no trouble staying glued to their screens to watch the market. Others would choose a less time-demanding option. Regardless of the methods used, if anyone from either of those groups enjoys trading, they can benefit from their preferred trading methods.

What Is Swing Trading?

Swing trading can be defined as trading that captures the gains on a stock over a few days or weeks. Remember how day traders are expected to complete a trading transaction in one day? In contrast, swing traders have no stipulated time frame. Instead, they can buy a stock when its price is low and hold off until there is an increase in its price before selling. This way, investors involved in swing trades can make massive profits based on the opportunity to hold their stock for relatively extended periods.

Swing trading often makes use of technical analysis to seek out trading opportunities.

Understanding Swing Trading

Traders who perform swing trades often buy stocks during a trading season and hold on to them over time until there is a rise in that stock in the market. Eventually, they can sell it and make a profit.

The point here is to take advantage of the increase in the price of a stock, be it foreign exchange stock or shares. Most traders seek out volatile stocks, which have a lot of movement, while others go for steady stocks. Swing traders' study and identify when an asset is likely to move up or down in value, so they cash in on this movement and make an exit when they should.

Swing traders use technical and fundamental analysis to monitor market trends. They also examine the risk-to-reward ratio.

Advantages of Swing Trading

Many benefits are attached to this type of trading because of certain factors, including time constraints and cost efficiency.

Time

It is important to note that because of the relatively extended time frame of swing trading, those who adhere to this method need not be glued to their computer screens at all times to watch the price performances of their chosen stock. Unlike day trading, which can be perceived as a full-time dedication to monitoring performances, swing traders can devote time to other essential tasks because they don't have to watch the market all the time. As such, they can take time off trading for a few days or weeks, barring any contingencies.

Benefiting From Longer Trends

To reiterate, swing traders benefit from longer trends, while day traders rely heavily on the short-term volatility of certain assets. Swing traders who perform analysis in a broader time spectrum are more likely to make sound and reliable evaluations that are not susceptible to false signals and noise.

Cost Efficiency

The cost of trading can be found in the spread between buying and selling securities. While day trading spreads are small, they get charged every time you trade, consuming some of the gains made by the investor.

For swing traders, the spread matters less since trades are placed over a longer time frame. The spread, which is usually only a few pips, gets charged less frequently and is smaller compared to the size of the overall profits made. If, however, a swing trader is still trading very often, like a day trader, then the spread will become a bigger factor.

Pros and Cons

Pros

- **It allows investors some spare time**: Swing trading is unlikely to considerably eat up a trader's time. With this method, you do not perpetually have to watch the market. Instead, you can enter and exit a trade after a few days or weeks.

- **It can be pretty profitable**: If you possess a good risk management technique, swing trades can be less stressful and beneficial. Also, if you consistently implement the required swing trading strategies, you can make good returns. An investor can make between 10% and 50% return on investment (ROI) yearly from swing trading, which is better than many other trading methods.

- **It does not tie down your capital for an extended period**: Unlike other long-term trading methods, investors do not have to be stuck with a bad stock for longer than necessary. Swing trading gives you greater flexibility to manage your funds so that at every point in time, these funds do the base work in ensuring a fruitful yield.

Cons

- **Exposure to weekend and midnight market risks**: Since swing traders often leave their trades running throughout the night, they may be affected by midnight market volatility.

- **Market timing is tricky**: It can be difficult to time the market no matter how experienced you are at trading.

- **The costs can add up**: Although swing trading is cheap, especially compared to day trading, the costs can still add up and do need to be accounted for.

Day Trading vs. Swing Trading

If you are a beginner investor venturing into the stock market, swing trading may be more profitable. But compared to performing a day trade, the financial rewards of swing trading are not always as substantial as investors hope.

Swing trading has a risk management technique referred to as the Kelly criterion. This technique is unpopular in the retail trading world but is much more prevalent in professional, institutional, and bank trading businesses. Practically, the Kelly criterion posits that when the outcome of any trade is highly uncertain, traders, historically, tend to double down on these positions in the hopes of a more rewarding result. In most cases, uncertain outcomes, especially those that appear to be skewed in favor of an investor, may cause them to feel less risk-averse and be willing to bet more of their capital. Swing traders make fewer trades but with greater assurance of profitability because of the fundamental analysis strategy involved.

Swing Trading Tactics

Trend Trading

This refers to trades set up after succinctly analyzing an asset's momentum and assessing its potential gains. Suffice it to say that trend trading is most efficient when the price movement of an asset is headed in an overall direction—either up or down.

In trend trading, investors tend to base their decision-making on the upward or downward movement of their preferred indicators. To identify upward trends, the indicators would show higher highs and higher lows. Conversely, you can make out downward trends with lower lows and lower highs.

Counter-Trend Trading

This is the opposite of trend trading. A counter-trend trader analyzes the market, recognizes the break from the trend before it happens, and tries to catch up with this prediction. It is vital to maintain steadfastness in circumstances where the price seems to move against you. However, if a trend becomes increasingly unfavorable, the investor should consider exiting to avoid more significant losses.

Understanding Indicators

Swing traders are often inclined to profit from the mini-trends that ensue between the highs and lows. To achieve this, there is a need to recognize new momentum as quickly as possible, hence the use of indicators. Indicators are used to identify trends and breakouts—the latter being a deviation from the trend.

The top five swing trade indicators include:

- **Moving averages**: This is used to calculate the mean of a market's price movement over a given time.

- **Volume**: This indicator provides an adequate understanding of the strength of a new trend.

- **Ease of movement**: With this indicator, traders can recognize if a comparatively low quantity of trades propels market movement.

- **Relative strength index (RSI)**: This indicator helps to determine if a swing might be on the horizon by showing whether a market is overbought or oversold.

- **Stochastic oscillator**: This indicator compares the closing price of a market to the range of its price over a given period.

Real-World Example

Arlie Peyton was a business teacher at both high schools and colleges before he retired early to join the trading world. He read books on swing trading, which helped him gain helpful insight into the market and achieve significant success as an investor.

In late 2014, the market was robust, and Peyton traded many popular stocks like NFLX, AMZN, ATVI, and MU and made a sizable profit from these investments. As a new trader, he did not buy more than five stocks at a time. He was trying to gain an in-depth understanding of these stocks, and the fewer they were, the easier this exercise would be.

Peyton also believed that if investors could strategically plan their entry and exit, they would make money from swing trading. And this is where fundamental analysis comes into play. Observing the growth of a company, he would say, is more critical than simply relying on technical analysis (Peyton, 2017).

According to Peyton, "trading is like playing a game of chess with a giant countdown timer in front of you the whole time." The goal is to get in at the right time, usually at the beginning of its upward trend, and get out at the right time, which is at the very beginning of its downward trend.

Key Takeaways

- Swing trading capitalizes on short-term to medium-term stock appreciation within weeks or days.

- One advantage of swing trading is that traders have enough time to enter and exit a trade, as it is not time-consuming. Swing trading may be less profitable compared to day trading, but it is less costly.

- Exposure to weekend and midnight gaps, the possibility

of missing out on exceptional stocks, difficulty in timing the market, and the possibility of the cost going up are some of the disadvantages of swing trading.

- Trend trading, counter-trend trading, and understanding indicators are some strategies used in swing trading.

A stock portfolio is essential for every investor. It serves as a framework to help you oversee your investments. In the next chapter, we will discuss this useful and imperative concept.

Chapter 10

Your Stock Portfolio

An individual investor should regularly act as an investor, not a speculator.

–Benjamin Graham

To safely keep a record of certain important events, some individuals possess journals or write on their phones. A portfolio serves a similar purpose as a record of all the investments operated by an investor. Through the portfolio, you can see how one type of security relates to its other assets. That is, whether there is a correlation or correlation is absent.

This chapter is going to take readers on a journey towards enlightenment, starting from what stock correlation is, positive versus negative correlation, the correlation coefficient, how to calculate stock correlation, why stock correlation matters for investors, diversification, making uncorrelated assets correlate, and how you can use correlation to develop and strengthen your portfolio.

What Is Stock Correlation?

Correlation, in layperson's terms, means the relationship between two variables. That said, the same knowledge will be used to describe what a stock correlation is. In a stock market analysis, investors tend to study the relationship between the varying types of stocks they purchase over time. To successfully monitor the relationship between these stocks, investors employ the strategies of stock correlation. They make deductions about the correlation of these stocks to each other by monitoring how one of the stocks outperforms or underperforms the other.

Stock correlation is a chart that shows the relationship between two stocks and their price movements. It can also represent the relationship between stocks and other financial securities like bonds and real estate. Correlation can either be positive or negative. It is positive when the assets move in the same direction on the chart, while it is considered negative when the stocks move in opposite directions.

Positive vs. Negative Stock Correlation

Relative to each other, stocks can either be positively or negatively correlated. On a correlation chart, each asset or variable is represented by an indicator. This indicator shows the upward or downward movement of the asset in the market. Generally, it shows when the price of an asset increases or decreases.

When the two assets move in tandem, it is considered a positive correlation. If one asset moves upward, the other is also moving closely upward. On the flip side, if one asset is moving downward, the other asset is likely to be moving downward as well. A positive correlation shows a product's demand in relation to its price. Note that a positive correlation does not have anything to do with benefits, as the term may imply. It only displays the relationship between two variables moving in the same direction. An instance of a positive correlation can be observed in the relationship between fuel and airlines. If there is an increase in fuel prices, there will also be an increase in plane tickets since planes need fuel to move.

A negative correlation is the opposite of a positive correlation, where two assets move in different directions. In statistics, a negative correlation is indicated by the value -1, where 0 is a correlation, and +1 is a positive correlation.

The Correlation Coefficient

The correlation coefficient is a calculation that reveals the similarities between two securities. Should they trend in a similar fashion, this would be a positive correlation. If they move in dissimilar directions, however, then this would be a negative correlation.

To show the strength of the relationship between two securities, correlation coefficients are expressed numerically as -1, 0, or +1.

How to Calculate Stock Correlation

The calculation for stock correlation is arguably a complex matter. However, this section will attempt to simplify it as much as possible.

Correlation can be calculated in several ways. The most common method used in calculating correlation is the Pearson product-moment method. This method calculates the linear relationship between two variables.

Here are the steps below:

1. Collect data for the "x" variable and the "y" variable.

2. Get the mean of the "x" variable and the "y" variable.

3. Deduct the mean of the "x" variable from each value of the "x" variable.

4. Subtract the mean of the "y" variable from each value of the "y" variable.

5. Multiply each of the differences between the "x" variable means and the "x" variable value by the corresponding difference related to the "y" variable.

6. Square each of these differences and sum up the outcome.

7. Determine the square root of the value obtained in Step 6 above.

8. Divide the value in step 5 by the value obtained in Step 7.

$R = n \times (summation(x, y) - (summation (x) \times summation(y))) \div \sqrt{n \times summation (x^2) - summation (x)^2} \times (n \times summation (y)^2 \, summation.$

Why Stock Correlation Matters for Investors

Correlation plays a vital role in finance because it foretells future trends and manages risks within a portfolio. It helps in creating and pricing derivatives as well as other complex financial instruments. Correlation is also essential for investors in managing their portfolios to measure the diversification among the securities contained in the portfolio. Modern portfolio theory measures the correlation of all securities in an investor's portfolio to deduce the most efficient frontier.

Diversification

Diversification is an important technique used by investors to avoid having their portfolios wiped out by one bad experience in the stock market. The saying "don't put all your eggs in one basket" applies to diversification. Here, investors vary their portfolios across different assets and companies, thereby protecting their funds. A diversified portfolio includes different securities like stocks, bonds, real estate, etc., which are diversified by buying shares from different companies.

The risk associated with having a portfolio containing one asset is higher than that of an investor with different holdings. When you diversify your investments, you mitigate the risks you are exposed to and can maximize profits. The risks here can be prevented and, as such, are unsystematic. Examples of systematic risks, on the other hand, include interest rates, recessions, pandemics, and wars.

Making Uncorrelated Assets Correlated

The absence of correlation between assets creates non-correlation. In correlation, two or more assets relate to each other, which means the assets are affected by the same factors. In positive correlation, if something happens in the market that leads to the fall of one asset, the other asset falls as well, and if it leads to the rise of one, the other rises. In a negative correlation, what causes an upward movement of one asset leads to a downward trend of the other. Non-correlated stocks are those whose values are not tied to significant oscillations in the traditional market.

Investors need to have some of these stocks to create a balance in their portfolios. Some non-correlating stocks include REITs and gems that can serve as investments. MPT emphasizes that investors should look for invariably uncorrelated assets to limit risk. This practically guarantees a diversified portfolio.

Using Correlation for Your Portfolio

How Does Hedging Work?

Hedging is a risk management strategy that investors, companies, and businesses employ to prevent losses in investments by taking different positions in related assets. Think of hedging as insurance. When people hedge, they insure themselves against the impact of an adverse event on their investments. Like in daily life, for instance, home insurance provides a hedge against the possibility of suffering severe financial losses due to fire outbreaks, robberies, and other unforeseen circumstances. Big companies like Kellogg's buy corn in large quantities to hedge against price fluctuations in the future. Portfolio managers, investors, and corporations use this technique to lower their portfolio's exposure to different risks.

It is a known fact that reducing risk, however minimally, will likely cause a decline in potential profits. Likewise, hedging reduces potential losses but does not increase potential profits.

Hedging Through Diversification

Diversification offers investors the opportunity to reduce risk across their portfolios. Using your knowledge of correlation would be very beneficial in setting up a diversified portfolio. That way, you can monitor uncorrelated assets and add them to your portfolio. This is like getting a portfolio mix of uncorrelated assets to prevent risks that could affect your investments.

Hedging, on the other hand, helps investors decrease their losses on an asset by taking an offsetting position in that asset. Trading offers different ways to hedge stock and options positions. People prefer diversification because it allows them to own multiple assets that do not rise and fall together. If an asset collapses, the investor won't suffer a total loss. An example is people who offset the risk of stock ownership by acquiring bonds.

Risks of Hedging

- It involves a cost that may significantly reduce profit.

- Since risks and rewards are directly proportional, reducing risks could lead to reduced profits.

- For short-term traders like day traders, hedging is complex to follow.

- Hedging offers very little profit when the market is moving well.

- Trading futures requires having higher account requirements, such as capital or balance.

- To successfully hedge your investments, you must have good trading skills since it is a trading strategy.

How to Trade Safe-Haven Assets

"Safe-haven" assets, as their name implies, offer protection from financial loss in the event of a downturn in the market. It is an investment that is required to increase in value when the market faces turbulence. Investors seek safe-havens to limit their vulnerability to losses during market downturns. So, investors and traders put their money in safe-haven assets to prevent losses. The most common safe-havens to trade are gold and defensive stocks.

In times of market downturns, assets that are viewed as safe-havens tend to outperform the majority of the market. Although investors use safe-havens to secure their money, traders have to use this opportunity to identify them, anticipate price movements, and implement strategies to maximize profits.

Examples of Safe-Haven Assets

A few popular safe-haven assets include the following:

- Gold
- Japanese Yen
- US Dollar
- Government Bond
- Swiss France
- Defensive Stocks

Gold

Gold is considered a safe-haven since the central bank's decisions cannot be manipulated by interest rates. Unlike paper currencies, gold cannot be influenced by actions like printing. A good example of gold being a safe-haven can be found in the

2008 financial crisis. The influx of investment increased to 24% in 2009 due to the increased price of gold. And it continued this upward movement till 2011.

Japanese Yen

The Japanese Yen is considered a safe-haven because it increases in value when U.S. dollars and government bonds experience fluctuations. It received this status due to Japan's high trade surplus compared to its debts.

US Dollar

The US dollar has consistently been a safe-haven during economic downturns for over fifty years now. This came about because of the 1944 Bretton Woods agreement, which introduced a fixed currency system that made the US dollar the world's primary reserve. Though this system has been abolished, the US dollar remains the world's largest economy.

Government Bonds

Government bonds are issued by the government of a particular state. Their status as a safe-haven results from the US government's credit status and the high quality of their income in dollars. Because of this, investors put their faith in them and buy bonds with the assurance of getting paid in full at maturity. Examples are Treasury bills and notes. Treasury bills have a maturity of one year or less, while Treasury bonds have a maturity rate of ten years.

Swiss Franc

The Swiss Franc appreciates whenever there is a global financial crisis. Investors favor Swiss accounts because of the neutrality of the Swiss government, the strength of their economy, and their well-developed banking sector.

Defensive Stocks

Defensive stocks are the securities of companies that provide goods and services like utilities, food, healthcare, etc. They are regarded as safe-havens. After all, they are likely to stay stable because they are constantly in demand.

Key Takeaway

- Correlation means the relationship between two assets in a stock portfolio.

- Correlation can be positive or negative. Non-correlated assets are suitable for diversification.

- Diversification protects the portfolio from risk.

- Hedging is a risk management technique to prevent acquiring losses from a market downturn.

- Safe-havens are where investors keep their money during a financial crisis.

The next chapter will highlight how you can make the most out of tax planning by reducing your tax rates to the barest minimum.

Chapter 11

Tax Planning

Many... investors could be overlooking another way to potentially add to their returns: tax efficiency.

—Fidelity Viewpoints

"Death and taxes" are the most common tax phrase there is. While other life factors may be uncertain, these two can always be expected to happen: death and the payment of taxes. The thought of paying taxes would not bring a smile to the face of any corporate worker or business owner, and I share this grim sentiment. After working all year to grow your wealth, one does not expect a sizable chunk of it to be extracted as tax. Although this is an understandable requirement, we still wish every last fruit of our labor would remain in our purses. But what if I told you that tax could be pictured as a game? And while the IRA makes up the game's rules, this should not diminish its excitement.

What if there is a chance that you could reduce the rate of your taxes in a way that is acceptable by the books? Does this catch your interest? Tax planning is focused on how to adequately and systematically map out ways to pay taxes without feeling or being shortchanged. A vast majority of people are still unknowingly paying more in taxes than they should, and this is because they are unaware of all the options available to reduce their taxable income.

In this chapter, we are going to be exploring taxes on investments.

Investment Taxes

Just as you pay taxes whenever you get your salaries, you also pay taxes on the returns of your investments. This is called an investment tax. It does not matter how long that asset has been in your portfolio. If it has moved into your account, brokerage or not, you'll be taxed on it. Investment taxes fall into two categories: income tax and CGT.

There are different kinds of investment income, including dividends, capital gains, and interest. You pay taxes on all of them as an investor. That is to say, as long as the money enters your domicile account, you owe the government a percentage of that cash. Some taxes are due when you trade investments for a gain.

Reduced Tax Burden

As an investor, you must pay attention to the tax rates associated with your specific investment portfolio. You may seek legal ways to decrease the money you have to pay the government.

Asset Placement

This is a tax-minimization strategy used by investors. It relies on the fact that not all assets are taxed the same. To profit from this strategy, you must have taxable and tax-deferred accounts. This way, you can benefit from both accounts.

Tax-conscious investors would place these investments in a taxable account to enjoy benefits like:

- Individual stocks they plan to hold for at least a year.
- Tax-managed stocks like ETFs and mutual funds.
- Qualified dividend stocks.
- Municipal bond funds.

They also place the investments listed below in their tax-advantaged or tax-deferred accounts, such as a 401(k):

- Individual stocks should be held for less than a year.
- Stock funds that reproduce short-term capital gains.
- Taxable bond funds.
- Real estate investment trusts.

Tax-Loss Harvesting

Tax-Loss Harvesting (TLH) is a strategy used to reduce taxes paid to the government by consciously selling an investment at a loss. It could also be used for personal income, tradable securities, and cryptocurrencies. This strategy is only relevant to taxable investment income, and it defers taxes but doesn't cancel them.

Some advocates posit that tax-loss harvesting is an effective way to protect one's investments from market volatility. However, critics warn that this method could backfire even for professionals (Kopp, 2022). It is advisable to consult the advice of an investment tax professional before venturing into this strategy.

Capital gains or losses are those additional profits or losses made from an investment. For instance, if the difference between the money paid for that asset and the price at which it was sold allows an investor to employ a tax-loss harvesting tool, they may deliberately sell their investments with zero profits to reduce their taxes.

Tax on Dividends

Dividends can be defined as profits or interests paid by companies to their stockholders for investing in their company. Dividends are paid periodically by the company to shareholders. Shareholders are required to pay taxes on the dividends paid to them. For tax, there are two types of dividends:

- Qualified dividends.
- Non-Qualified or ordinary dividends.

Qualified dividends have the advantage of lower tax rates. In contrast, nonqualified dividends have a much higher tax rate.

How can you identify an eligible dividend?

1. A US corporation or a qualifying foreign entity, issue qualified dividends.

2. It is counted as a dividend by IRS standards. Other phenomena are called dividends but are not recognized as dividends. Some of them are premiums from insurance companies, the annual distribution given by credit unions to their members, capital gains, or that which is gotten from tax-exempt organizations.

3. You hold the security for an extended period. This means that the securities have been held for more than 60 days during the 121 days.

Tax on Interest

Whenever you earn interest on your investments, you are most likely to pay taxes on them, no matter how little. This is because they would be recognized as regular income by federal tax standards.

Your tax rate depends on factors such as income level and deductibles. And because these variables change, your tax rate may change as well.

Examples of interests that are taxable:

- **Federal bonds**: Although treasury bonds are not taxable at state and local levels, it is taxable on your federal tax returns. The interest you earn on Treasury bonds, savings bonds, and corporate bonds is all taxable.

- **Mutual funds**: Whatever interest you earn on mutual funds is taxable, except for those in tax-deferred accounts like 401(k) and IRA.

- **CDs and interest-bearing accounts**: Your interest on CDs (certificates of deposits), money market accounts, and deposit accounts such as checking and savings accounts are taxable.

- The value of gifts, including those for opening an account, is taxable.

- The interest you get from loaning money to other people, you have to pay tax on.

Tax on Capital Gains

Tax on Capital Gains: Long-Term vs. Short-Term

Short-term and long-term gains are the lengths of time you have held onto and profited from an asset. Short-term gains are twelve months or less, while long-term gains are above twelve months.

Capital gains refer to the net gain one gets from selling an asset. How much a person must remit for capital gains tax is relative to their holding period, net profit, income, and filing status. While the tax on short-term capital gains is similar to regular income, such as wages from a job, long-term capital gains are filed differently from regular income.

If you make a long-term capital gain (more than twelve months), chances are that your tax remittance will not be significant. This means that you could enjoy a little break from paying taxes if you can hold on to your assets for a little longer than a year. For instance, if you buy 100 shares from a company at $20 per share and sell them later at $50 per share, and your regular income is $100,000 a year, you will pay $450 if you made a long-term investment. But if you'd instead make a short-term investment, your tax would be charged at the standard rate.

However, net investment taxes apply both to short-term gains and long-term gains. This means that if, as a single filer, your gross income is more than $200,000, and as a joint filer, it's more than $250,000, you have to pay an additional net investment income tax of exactly 3.8%.

There are certain states in the US where you are not required to pay taxes on capital gains. States like: Wyoming, Washington, Texas, Tennessee, South Dakota, New Hampshire, Nevada, Florida, and Alaska.

Use Investment Capital Losses to Offset Gains

If you are familiar with this, you would know that you can offset capital gains using investment capital losses. However, to make the most out of this tax benefit, you have to figure out a way to deduct capital losses in the most tax-efficient way possible. The US tax law provides that only realized capital gains can influence your income tax bill. Therefore, if you hold on to a stock loss without selling it before the year runs out, it would not be counted as a tax deduction for the previous year. This provides some comfort for investors when they have stock losses.

Capital losses, just like capital gains, are categorized into short-term and long-term losses. The former refers to stocks kept for less than twelve months, and the latter exceeds twelve months.

When you take a short-term capital loss, you get a deduction. This is because long-term losses are figured at the same low tax rate as long-term capital gains.

Tax Losses and Wash Sales

Some people sell their stocks at the end of the year to get a tax deduction and repurchase them the following year. If you were thinking about doing that, you might want to reevaluate this decision.

A particular law forbids people from doing that. It is called the wash-sale rule. This sale prevents investors who sell at a loss from repurchasing the same investment within 61 days and claiming tax benefits. The rule also applies to most assets one can hold in brokerage accounts, such as bonds, ETFs, mutual funds, and options. The penalty is that you cannot use the loss to offset gains, nor can you reduce your taxable income. Although this can be tricky, one way to avoid the wash-sale rule is to replace your investments with mutual funds or ETFs.

Hold the Shares Inside an IRA, 401(k), or Other Tax-Advantaged Account

Tax-advantaged accounts, unlike brokerage accounts, are also tax-deferred. They include IRAs and 401(k) plans. This means you don't need to pay taxes on any money that goes into these accounts unless you withdraw it. The school of thought behind this strategy is that by the time you access the money put in those accounts, your tax rates will be relatively lower than they are now.

These accounts have annual contribution limits. That is, per year, there are limits to the amount of cash you can put in there. For instance, you can only contribute $6,000 to your IRA and $7,000 if you are fifty years of age or older. Although there is now an increase of $500 to your annual contribution limit starting in 2023. Investing your money in these tax-advantaged accounts not only helps you prepare a retirement plan but also helps you invest and save money in a tax-efficient way, allowing you to keep more of your investment profits than you would in a taxable account.

Key Takeaways

- Investment taxes are the money you owe the government for every investment you make.
- Asset placements can reduce your tax burden if you know how to play your cards right.

- You can save yourself some percentage of tax by selling your investment at a loss.

- Some tax-advantaged accounts, including IRAs and 401(k), are primarily used as retirement plans. It's a win-win.

Chapter 12

Strategies for Mitigating Risk

Successful investing is about managing risk, and not avoiding it.

–Benjamin Graham

The primary goal of most people in the business world is to manage the odds since risks are generally inevitable. Investors mitigate risk by buying and holding on to a few stocks for a long time to reduce the chances of losing. While this strategy works to an extent, it does not entirely protect investors from losing money.

The following are strategies that you can implement to shield your investment portfolio from failure:

- **Long-term treasuries**: These treasuries, like bonds, can be considered defensive assets for many reasons. Historically, they were utilized by institutional investors as one of the most liquid securities in the world. One reason is that in times of great crisis, long-term treasuries have served as a haven because of their risk-free attributes. Suffice it to say that under circumstances where there is a decline in the stock market and the economic slowdowns negatively impact the performance of the price, the long-term characteristics of the Treasury help to mitigate risks and strengthen the defense. It is advisable to invest in long-term treasuries because this type of mitigation helps you simplify and generate income periodically.

- **Keeping up with trends**: This process is strategic and systematic. It depends on certain factors like interest rates, equities, government bonds, and commodities, among others. The essence of following trends as a medium for mitigating risk is to become aware of the direction of trends or particular moments in the market that highlight how well or how badly a stock has performed in the past to accurately predict its future performance.

In the absence of this risk-management strategy, as an investor, you are most likely to struggle with the market during inflections and volatile market environments. The good thing about this is that it is not selective. That is, there is no bias as to whether the investment is short- or long-term. Instead, it is wired to capture upward and downward price trends accordingly by shorting the assets. Over time, keeping up with trends has become an effective strategy for mitigating risks as it tends to exhibit low correlations that coincide with other traditional investments and equities.

- **Long volatility**: Long volatility as a strategy is quite flexible regarding the maturity time of a stock purchased. Generally, this strategy benefits from rising volatility in the underlying investment classes, while calm markets induce losses.

- **Understand your risk tolerance**: One of the most underrated abilities to possess as an investor is an understanding of how much risk you can endure. This factor may be strongly dependent on age and present financial obligations. It is often said that younger investors can bear more risks than older investors because they are, quite often, single or without children, thus having fewer financial responsibilities.

- **Diversify**: The diversification strategy is an integral part of managing and sustaining a portfolio. After you have carefully selected your choice of the perfect mix of asset classes, risk can be mitigated by diversifying the investment. An excellent example of this is if you decide to invest in a mutual fund portfolio. To diversify your assets, you may invest in large, middle, and small cap mutual funds. By doing so, if the market suffers a decline and prices are affected, spreading your investments in this manner may provide a hedge against financial loss.

- **Due diligence**: One saving grace in investment is performing your due diligence. You cannot successfully mitigate any risk, whether big or small, if you do not study the market before diving in, as it were. For example, it is your responsibility to do a concrete fundamental analysis of the company you are investing in to predict how well it will perform in the future. It is never advisable to invest in stocks for the simple reason that someone encouraged you to do so. To avoid losses, keep an open mind regardless of the recommendation and conduct your research.

- **Never follow the herd**: Warren Buffett once said that "the most significant quality for an investor is disposition, not intellect. You need a disposition that neither derives great pleasure from being with the masses nor against them." Most investors are easily swayed by the things that look like "big opportunities" or "the new wave." You must learn and develop the habit of taking a step back to assess the situation closely and weigh the possible risks when the market takes a dip in the future. You should be able to ascertain whether you are merely following the crowd or making calculated decisions based on thorough evaluation and personal research. This strategy helps to counter unforeseen risks that could lead to losses. Know your risk capacity, ensure you can determine the suitability of the investment, and refuse to jump on the bandwagon to purchase any stock.

- **Don't gamble; research**: Prudent investment is separate from gambling. Investing requires tactical study and evaluation to make a choice. Without these, you might be plunged into a well of failure and disappointment. It is wrong to take wild predictions or risks. Ensure that you study the market, the stock prices, and, most importantly, the financial health of the company in which you are investing. All of these are essential factors to consider when making investments. Also, evaluate the company's stocks well enough to understand their intrinsic value.

The objective is to find a good balance between risks and returns without jeopardizing the latter. As soon as you can guarantee the implementation and efficacy of these practical strategies, ensure that you do a periodic check on and review the performances of the market. Review it regularly to ensure that it is still effective, and you are on the right track with your personal finance goals. It also helps to reduce the chances of you being carried away by emotions in your decision-making processes.

Key Takeaways

- Risks are inevitable. What matters the most is the implementation of the strategies regarding how they can be managed to minimize impact.

  Risks are inevitable. What matters the most is the implementation of the strategies regarding how they can be managed to minimize impact.

- Seek professional help from reliable financial experts in situations where you feel lost or unable to navigate through an investment process. Do not let a poor performer weigh you down. Investment is a process, and you should view it as such.

Risk mitigation is an integral aspect of investing, whether as a beginner or an expert. It is vital not to undermine the influence of money management skills when venturing into the finance world. The next chapter will entail the acquisition of money management skills, their importance, and the principles guiding their implementation.

Chapter 13

Money Management

You should not save what is remaining after spending. Instead, spend what is left after saving.

—Warren Buffett

Money management, while an essential financial skill, is also generally necessary to help anyone navigate the ups and downs of life. It can be difficult to correctly predict what life has in store for you regarding your finances. As such, it is prudent to make provisions for contingencies that could mean the difference between financial stability and bankruptcy.

This chapter seeks to shed light on what money management is when it comes to securing a diversified investment portfolio. The importance, as well as the benefits, will be distinctively checked out in this chapter. You should also pay extra attention to aspects that might require you to become more practical and take action steps to become a better version of yourself financially.

What Does the Term Money Management Imply?

Money management, as the term implies, can be defined as creating a budget, saving, investing funds, or spending in a calculated manner to maintain financial security. In other words, it highlights the capital usage of an individual and how he manages the inflows and outflows of funds. In this case, money management is regarded as managing an investment portfolio effectively.

The concept of money management in the investment industry is quite broad. You may be familiar with the idea of individual investors or corporations seeking the expertise of financial advisors to aid in the proper management of their investment portfolio. It can be a tedious task to manage every aspect of one's finances single-handedly. Professional financial advisors can offer the needed support to help individuals and businesses manage their money.

The Importance of Money Management

It is not news that the financial market is growing exponentially. Fortunately, technology has matured to help anyone efficiently manage every aspect of their finances. The fundamental truth is that without proper management of your finances, it feels like a shield is placed over them—everything becomes a mystery. You might find yourself in situations where you have no idea how you spent a certain amount of money. You may also realize that you are living paycheck to paycheck. There are no savings, no emergency funds, and neither can you exactly point out a tangible purchase.

The importance of money management stems from the ability to have control over your finances and become familiar with how to handle the outflow of your income in a much better way to improve your financial status. People with little or no control over their finances tend to move around in an endless, repetitive cycle of economic stagnation or decline. The importance of money management as a personal skill and in the corporate world cannot be overemphasized. If it cannot be acquired as a beginner investor, you can seek the service of financial advisors who can help manage your finances adequately.

Principles of Money Management

Many books have been written, and millions of speeches have been given by financial educators on money management and how to acquire it as a skill. Each text and speech seems to possess the keys and principles that can help improve everyone's financial situation. This begs the question: Why do so many people still struggle with money management? It seems that economic liberation and success are codes that only a select few have been able to crack.

Financial management is not limited to making or saving money. It's also concerned with how one handles cash flow, personally or as an individual investor. The good thing is that with the right strategy and its due implementation, you can build up your wealth and achieve your investment goals with ease. The following are principles that will start you on the journey to gaining financial prosperity:

- **Draft a unique financial plan that aligns with your goals**: The first step to achieving financial success is to know what you want and how you hope to achieve it. An investment mistake that people make is to give in to the fear of missing out, abbreviated as FOMO. People with this habit tend to suffer more losses than they make actual gains.

- **Intelligently invest on a long-term basis**: The underlying idea of money management transcends the "earn" and "spend" routine. It all depends on your financial goals, your risk appetite, and your chosen assets. There are many options to select from as long as you are not looking to make immediate profits or overnight returns on the capital invested. An intelligent investment requires you to invest on a long-term basis by giving your money enough time—about three to seven years—to grow in the market. Most people fail to realize that investments are not a form of gambling. It requires due diligence, patience, and great discipline to generate the actual yields of your expectations.

  Most people fail to realize that investments are not a form of gambling

- **Plan professionally for your future**: As the common saying goes, "if you fail to plan, you plan to fail." To live a prudent life, you must develop foresight.

- **Set realistic goals**: The truth you're unlikely to hear from so-called financial professionals is that managing money and growing one's wealth can be tricky and arduous. At some point, if care is not taken, you may lose track of reality and embrace a tainted vision when investing. No one particularly enjoys losing money, but you may sabotage your progress if you do not remain practical in your decision-making process. Therefore, it is vital that, as a beginner investor, you take baby steps and, through practice, can gain the necessary skills and experience to win consistently.

- **Diversify**: You may already know that investing, as well as managing funds, requires logic instead of emotions. You should never put your eggs in a basket, no matter how right it feels. There will always be risks involved in the process. As such, you should consider investing in multiple asset classes.

Key Takeaways

- Money management refers to using an individual, household, or corporation's records to administer finances.

- Without good money management skills, an individual or company may be trapped in a cycle of bad financial outcomes and debt.

- Through the aid of technology in creating mobile apps and the emergence of financial advisors, individuals can manage their finances better.

The next chapter analyzes the concept of cash flow and how it can help investors sustain and grow their portfolios.

Chapter 14

Cash Flow

Do not ever take your eyes off the cash flow because it is the lifeblood of business.

—Sir Richard Branson

Cash flow, as the name implies, is the amount of money that goes in and out of an investment process. It is safe to say that when you have a positive flow of cash, it means that you have a healthy channel for generating funds as opposed to a negative cash flow, where a higher level of spending is observed. You may believe that the latter is a bad thing. But this might be a good thing if the money spent is being invested.

What Is Cash Flow?

In simple terms, the money received by a company is referred to as an "inflow," while the amount spent is referred to as an "outflow." This back-and-forth movement of money within an organization is called cash flow.

Let's say that company Q takes in revenue from the sales department and spends the cash on things like renovating the building structure and creating extensive offices. Let's also say that company Q generates income from investments made in other companies, including royalties and other licensing agreements. You can tell that company Q is edging toward a positive flow because its liquid assets are on the rise. It is capable of paying off expenses, reinvesting in its business affairs, paying its respective shareholders, and making provisions for a solid buffer against unforeseen financial difficulties.

Often, the cash flow of a corporation is determined by analysts through a standard financial statement. This analysis helps investors and the company's management discern its cash usage over time.

Categories of Cash Flow

Cash flow can be divided into three categories:

- **Operating cash flow**: This is determined by usual business operations. That is, cash generated from sales and money spent over certain operational business expenses like salaries and overhead.

- **Cash flows from financing**: This accentuates the cost of raising capital. For example, when a corporation issues a bond, shares, or a loan, the cash flow from financing highlights the details of the transactions to show the relationship between the number of bonds issued and the money being dispensed to sort out the company's expenses.

- **Cash flows from investments**: This refers to the amount spent on purchasing securities such as stocks and bonds designed to be held together in an investment portfolio.

Importance of Cash Flow From Investing

The premise of this chapter is to show the correlation between cash flow and investing. The importance of cash flow can be seen in how a corporation allocates cash over the long term. Say a company invests in fixed assets like real estate properties and equipment to enhance the development of its business. This may seem like a negative cash flow, given that the company is spending a considerable sum on these investments. But there's another way to consider this situation. Chances are that the assets that seem to be taking a lot out of the company's pockets at a specific time may pay off soon when the proceeds begin to come in. It is safe to say that companies may invest in long-term assets that will yield enough profits to make up for the outflow of cash.

Key Takeaways

- Cash flow is the activity of finances within a company; cash generated is known as an "inflow," and cash spent is an "outflow."

- A cash flow is categorized into three areas, namely: operations, financing, and investing.

- Managing cash flow is vital to investors when analyzing a company to determine whether it is a good investment or not.

Conclusion

The easiest way to manage your money is to take it one step at a time and not worry about being perfect.

–Ramit Sethi

Investments are a great way to kickstart a dependable and lasting financial journey. It is typically not a day's or a month's work. It takes consistency, the will to learn, dedication to trying the lessons learned, and, more importantly, discipline. As stated, multiple times in this book, no investment is risk-free. You have to take into consideration your risk tolerance level. For instance, how much can you bear to lose as an investor if the tides change?

> Investments are a great way to kickstart a dependable and lasting financial journey.

This book has succinctly and successfully analyzed the fundamentals of investments for anyone at the beginner level. In this book, stocks were studied in great detail. We also learned about the types of stocks and how each functioned. Charts, metrics, and tables were shown to be indicators that can help investors understand the behavior of stocks and other assets.

In the first chapter, we considered how demand and supply

determine the performance of stock prices in the market. We also learned that asset classes, in general, are varied. They include bonds, ETFs, mutual funds, real estate investment trusts (REITs), and index funds. Each portfolio has similarities and unique characteristics that set them apart.

It is essential to pay extra attention to the economic factors that influence the stock market. As stated earlier, investing requires analysis and strategic thinking. World-renowned investors like Warren Buffett, George Soros, and Elon Musk, among a long list of others, did not succeed as investors by making wild guesses. They were tactical and strategic. You should emulate this positive attitude toward investing and practice the various investment strategies discussed in this book.

Subsequent chapters examined topics like value investing, growth stocks, the basics of day trading, and the strategies employed by day traders to make consistent profits. It also highlighted the similarities and differences between day trading and swing trading, including the meaning and effect of "correlation" as a relationship between two assets in a stock portfolio.

In many cases, non-correlated assets are the best choice for a diversified portfolio because they are great risk management strategies. In the same chapter, we also examined the vitality of safe-haven assets as an opportunity for investors to save their money amid a financial crisis.

In the final chapter, we carefully studied investment taxes. This chapter highlighted the possibility of reducing the taxes you're expected to remit to the government.

Rome, as the saying goes, was not built in a day. As such, do not expect to achieve the same results as seasoned investors. Instead, be focused on learning nonstop. Widen your knowledge base and have fun while you're at it.

I hope that this book has equipped you with all of the necessary information that you seek to kickstart your investment journey. You should now have the right amount of zeal and resilience to weather the low tides of the stock market and be committed to practicing the steps provided in this book.

Glossary

Analysis: A meticulous examination of a thing or process.

Asset: A valuable property that is likely to retain its value if saved and may appreciate.

Capital: This refers to funds that may be used to start a business or acquire assets.

Diversify: To increase the number of one's investments and make them more varied.

Equity: This refers to the value of the shares that are sold by a business.

Intrinsic: To be a natural part of something.

Liability: A property that is unlikely to retain its value over time.

Momentum: The increasing force that is gained as a process develops.

Portfolio: This refers to the totality of an individual's or organization's investments.

Revenue: This refers to the substantial income made by an organization or state.

Risk: A situation in which an individual, organization, or state is made vulnerable to danger.

Tax: A compulsory levy on an individual's income and an organization's profits enforced by the government.

Value: This is an approximation of a property's worth, often in monetary terms.

References

Adam Messina quotes. (n.d.). Good Reads. https://www.goodreads.com/author/quotes/22431854.Adam_Messina

An essential options trading guide. (2022, August 19). Investopedia. https://www.investopedia.com/options-basics-tutorial-4583012

Best trading insights from Ed Seykota. (n.d.). Investopaper. https://www.investopaper.com/news/best-trading-insights-from-ed-seykota/

Daly, L. (2022). *These 3 tips from ramit sethi changed how I think about money.* The Ascent. https://www.fool.com/the-ascent/personal-finance/articles/these-3-tips-from-ramit-sethi-changed-how-i-think-about-money/

Dhoke, M. (2022, April 29). *5 investment lessons you should learn from Mr Benjamin Graham.* Personal FN. https://www.personalfn.com/dwl/financial-planning/5-investment-lessons-you-should-learn-from-mr-benjamin-graham

Folgers, J. (n.d.). *Tips for stock charts that enhance your analysis.* Investopedia. https://www.investopedia.com/articles/trading/10/high-performance-charts.asp

Folger, J. (2021, July 3). *Investing vs. trading: what's the difference?* Investopedia. https://www.investopedia.com/ask/answers/12/difference-investing-trading.asp

Gordon, B. (2021, July 30). *A strategy for trading options on index ETFs.* Expensivity. https://www.expensivity.com/a-strategy-for-trading-options-on-index-etfs/

Gupta, G. (2020). *Ensuring business survival with "cash flow."* LinkedIn. https://www.linkedin.com/pulse/ensuring-business-survival-cash-flow-gaurav

Hollands, J. (2000). *"Know what you own and know why you own it."* The Guardian.

Hopkins, J. (2021). *Seth Klarman: the greatest challenge for value investors.* The Acquirer's Multiple. https://acquirersmultiple.com/2021/06/seth-klarman-the-greatest-challenge-for-value-investors/

How does the law of supply and demand affect the stock market?. (2019). Investopedia. https://www.investopedia.com/ask/answers/040215/how-does-law-supply-and-demand-affect-stock-market.asp

Hugo's Way. (n.d.). *"I will tell you how to become rich. Close the doors, be fearful when others are greedy. Be greedy when others are fearful" – Warren Buffett*. Hugo.

Hugo's Way. (n.d.). *The goal of a successful trader is to make the best trades. Money is secondary – Alexander Elder*. Hug. https://hugosway.com/the-goal-of-a-successful-trader-is-to-make-the-best-trades-money-is-secondary-alexander-elder/

Hur, J. (2018, December 4). *History of the stock market - from the beginning to present time*. BeBusinessed.com. https://bebusinessed.com/history/history-of-the-stock-market/

Kikorangii, K. (2021, May 10). *Establishment of the stock market*. Investify. http://investify.co.nz/establishment-of-the-stock-market/

Kopp, M. C. (2022, July 4). H*ow tax-loss harvesting works for average investors*. Investopedia. https://www.investopedia.com/articles/taxes/08/tax-loss-harvesting.asp

Margin of safety: explained. (n.d.). Casual. https://www.causal.app/define/margin-of-safety

Nineteen best Philip Fisher quotes on investing. (n.d.). Investopaper. https://www.investopaper.com/news/best-philip-fischer-quotes/

Peyton, A. (2017, December 15). *I took a couple years off of work to swing trade. Here's what happened.* Medium. https://medium.com/the-ascent/i-took-a-couple-years-off-of-work-to-swing-trade-heres-what-happened-fbaa53087f3

Price, M. (2021, September 13). *How are stock prices determined?.* The Motley Fool. https://www.fool.com/investing/how-to-invest/stocks/how-are-stock-prices-determined/

Short sale: definition, example, risks, and margin requirements. (2021, January 28). Investopedia. https://www.investopedia.com/terms/s/shortsale.asp

Smigel, L. (2022, April 27). *History of the stock market.* Analyzing Alpha. https://analyzingalpha.com/stock-market-history

Six Best George Soros Quotes on Successful Investing. Read more at. (2023). Fincash. https://www.fincash.com/l/investment/george-soros-quotes-on-successful-investing

"The goal of a successful trader is to make the best trades. Money is secondary" – Alexander Elder. (n.d.). Hugo's Way. https://hugosway.com/the-goal-of-a-successful-trader-is-to-make-the-best-trades-money-is-secondary-alexander-elder/#:~:text=%22The%20goal%20of%20a%20successful,%22%20%2D%20Alexander%20Elder%20%2D%20Hugo%20FX

Understanding bonds and their risks. (n.d.). Merrill Edge. https://www.merrilledge.com/article/understanding-bonds-and-their-risks

Wolfson A. (2022). *Warren Buffett says this is the 'biggest mistake' people make with their money (and psst: it has to do with savings).* Market Watch. https://www.marketwatch.com/picks/warren-buffett-says-this-is-the-biggest-mistake-people-make-with-their-money-and-psst-it-has-to-do-with-savings-01659574976

What value investing is, and isn't. (2013). Safal Niveshak. https://www.safalniveshak.com/what-value-investing-is-and-isnt/

www.ingramcontent.com/pod-product-compliance
Lightning Source LLC
Chambersburg PA
CBHW031626210526
45464CB00004B/1769